CONTENTS

Biddy Baxter and **Edward Barnes**
devised and wrote the
Blue Peter Book

£2·50

HELLO

Do you recognise any of these photographs? They've all been in Blue Peter.

This year we're celebrating a double anniversary – Blue Peter's Silver Jubilee and twenty years of Blue Peter Books! That's what our competition's all about and you'll find the covers of all our annuals at the front and back of this 20th edition.

If you're one of the few people who have the very first Blue Peter Book you'll notice some interesting coincidences – five of our greatest friends are in books number One *and* Twenty! They're George Cansdale, the world-famous zoologist – Tim (William Timyn) the Sculptor and cartoonist – Margaret Parnell, who invents practically everything we make on the programme – Bob Broomfield, who illustrates our stories – and Dorothy Smith, the historian who writes for us as well as for the Blue Peter Special Assignments and Treasure Houses. Between them, these five people have provided thousands of Blue Peter items that have delighted and entertained millions of viewers, and we send them our special thanks in this Anniversary Book.

The message at the front of Book Number One said: "Don't forget, this is your programme." That's just as true today as it ever was. Our second vote of thanks goes to all our viewers over the years who've helped to make Blue Peter a Top Children's Programme – if it wasn't for all your interesting letters and good ideas, Blue Peter wouldn't exist!

By the time this book is published, Sarah will have begun her new career as an actress. Her three years on Blue Peter have gone in a flash, and some of the highlights of her last year on the programme are featured here – hot air ballooning, behind-the-scenes at the Royal Opera House, her transformation into Queen Elizabeth I, and her day with the Chelsea Pensioners, are amongst them all.

Just like Sarah, Janet Ellis was a Blue Peter viewer. Janet watched the programme in the days of Valerie Singleton and Christopher Trace, but little did she think then that one day she'd be in front of the cameras in the Blue Peter studio – perhaps that's what's going to happen to someone reading this 20th Book! We're delighted to welcome Janet to the team and you can find out about her audition on page 44.

The saddest happening of the past year has been the death of Jill, our silver spotted tabbie. Jill had taken part in nearly 600 editions of Blue Peter, and it was a tremendous shock to all of us when she died of heart failure on the morning of May 30th. Jill hadn't been in any pain before she died and had enjoyed seven very happy years on the programme.

An important date to remember is October 17th. That's when we'll be celebrating our 25th Birthday, so be sure not to miss the programme. By then there'll have been 1861 Blue Peters, and the people who've taken part have included the Queen, Princes and Princesses, famous sportsmen and women, pop stars, magicians, His Holiness the Pope, the Archbishop of Canterbury, the men who conquered Everest and the North & South Poles, explorers, around-the-world sailors and hundreds and thousands of Blue Peter viewers. If you keep on sending in your requests and ideas, we'll be all set for another celebration. It'll be in the year 2008 – our Golden Jubilee!

Simon Groom · Peter Duncan · Janet Ellis · Sarah Greene x

George · Jack · Goldie

1

2

THERE!

Turn to page 76 for the answers.

SILVER

October 16th, 1958
Leila Williams was Blue Peter's first girl presenter.

Christopher Trace and Valerie Singleton with Petra – Blue Peter's first-ever dog.

1962 and the programme's first Appeal was for parcels of toys.

Squeezing twenty-five years of Blue Peter into six pages of this book is like trying to pour the Niagara Falls into a milk jug!

It's easy to say the very first Blue Peter was televised on Monday, 16th October, 1958, with Christopher Trace and Leila Williams, and that ten presenters and thirteen pets later, we're celebrating our 25th Birthday in 1983 with Simon, Peter, Janet, Goldie, Jack and George. But describing all that's happened in between would fill a whole library of books.

In 1958, no one ever thought Blue Peter would last longer than six or eight weeks. The Head of Children's Programmes for BBC TV asked one of his producers, John Hunter Blair, to devise a programme that would fill fifteen minutes once a week. John had a think. His great passion was model railways – especially OO gauge – and he knew girls were keen on dolls, so he asked a blonde beauty queen called Leila Williams, who'd just won the title

JUBILEE

"Miss Great Britain 1957", to show the dolls, and an actor called Christopher Trace to run trains on a layout in the studio.

Very sadly, John became seriously ill and left the programme. Shortly afterwards he died. The weekly Blue Peter had a small but steady audience, and it didn't cost very much to put on, so there it stayed, and no one took a lot of notice of it. Leila Williams left after she married a member of a pop group called *The Mudlarks* and a young announcer called Valerie Singleton took her place. All kinds of producers looked after Blue Peter, none of them for any great length of time, but in 1962 a junior member of Children's Programmes Department, Edward Barnes, was asked to help Biddy Baxter, the new producer who'd been appointed to take over Blue Peter.

1962 was to prove to be a key year in Blue Peter's history – changes took place that were to have long-lasting effects.

Petra's eight puppies were born on September 9th, **1965**.

John Noakes looked after Patch, one of Petra's puppies.

George Cansdale with Lady Sarah Armstrong-Jones and Prince Edward.

To get viewers to send in their ideas, it was decided to have a badge that could be won for interesting letters and suggestions. The programme was to have a symbol, and the young artist, Tony Hart, came up with the now famous Blue Peter ship. And Edward had the idea of having a puppy on the programme.

The 1960s was the time that huge high-rise flats were being built all over Britain. Pets were forbidden. There were hundreds of thousands of children who could never have a dog of their own. On the last Blue Peter before Christmas, 1962, a large cardboard box covered

◁ Jason, Blue Peter's first cat, was a Seal Point Siamese.

with Christmas paper and ribbons was presented to Christopher Trace and Valerie Singleton. When they opened it up, there was an eight-week old brown and black mongrel puppy. Right from the start, the idea was that the puppy would appear on every programme – not just the ones about dog training. She would be part of the team, and be a substitute pet for all the children who couldn't keep animals.

The day after the presentation, disaster struck. The un-named puppy, who'd been specially chosen by a vet, died. What could be done? The poor pup had only made one appearance, but the youngest viewers would be dreadfully upset to hear it had died, so the decision was taken to

Peter Purves, from *Dr Who*, joined the programme in 1967. ▷

find a substitute. There was no time to consult any vet. There was a dash to the nearest pet shop, and by a strange co-incidence, there in the window was a brown and black mongrel puppy. No one knew anything about its background, or whether or not it had had its injections. But the little puppy who was eventually called "Petra" by Blue Peter viewers, must have been pretty healthy, because she appeared on the programme for fifteen years until she died on September 14th, 1977.

By then, Rosemary Gill, who later became the Editor of *Multi-*

◁ The hilarious moment when Lulu the elephant took over the studio.

Coloured Swap Shop, joined the Production Team, and Blue Peter's audience had grown to eight million viewers. Petra's photograph appeared in all the national newspapers and every news bulletin on radio and TV carried a report of her death. By the end of the week, 20,000 letters of sympathy had been received in the Blue Peter office. The truth is that Petra was owned by all those millions of people who were saddened by her death.

John Noakes was the first civilian in Britain to make a 5-mile free-fall jump.

1971. Valerie Singleton and Princess Anne filming Blue Peter Royal Safari.

The other important 1962 development was the start of the Blue Peter Appeals. Up until then there'd been a tradition that every Christmas the studio was filled with toys, like a huge advertisement, so that viewers could decide what presents they would ask for. Biddy, Edward and Rosemary thought it might be an idea to point out that some children would be having a pretty miserable Christmas with no presents at all, so the programme appealed for gifts of toys. The Target was 10 sacksful, but

In June **1971** we buried a box full of souvenirs of the programme and planted our Tree for the Year 2000.

Measuring our Tree with Lesley Judd and Shep, the Border Collie. In the year 2000 the presenters of Blue Peter can dig up the box and reveal its contents.

Daniel, the Blue Peter baby, made TV history by being the first baby ever to appear regularly on a programme.

hundreds of parcels arrived, enough to help children in need all over Britain. After that, the idea snowballed, and, ever since, help has been given to a good cause once a year.

Surprising as it may seem, the idea is *not* to raise the maximum amount of money, but to enable every single viewer who watches Blue Peter to take part, no matter how badly off they are. That's why we ask for waste commodities rather than cash. And because we believe very firmly that charity doesn't begin at home, we always divide our Appeals between good causes at home and abroad. All the suggestions that are sent to the programme throughout the year are considered very carefully indeed, and we try to choose the particular good cause that most viewers want to support.

By 1962 the programmes were 25 minutes long, and in 1964 it was decided to put Blue Peter on twice a week. Christopher Trace said there was far too much to do for just two presenters, so a lively young man called John Noakes joined the team. John was an actor from Halifax, who'd started life as an aircraft fitter. For the first two years on the programme John's great disadvantage was not being able to remember his words! But he was a terrific dare-devil, and one of his most memorable Blue Peter films showed him having a go in a very big way!

The Re-Naming Ceremony of the restored 532 Blue Peter – the Class A-2 Pacific Loco – in November **1970**.

By 1973, the RAF's crack parachute team asked John if he would like to make a five-mile free fall jump. After months of special training, John made his "long fall" and achieved three firsts: he became the first civilian in Britain to make a five-mile high free fall; he was the first outsider ever to join the Flying Falcons; and he was the first TV presenter in Britain to talk to a camera while falling through space.

In 1967 Christoper Trace decided to leave TV to become a writer, and Peter Purves took his place. Peter also took over looking after Petra, and she lived with him until shortly before her death. By now there was a Blue Peter cat – Jason – a beautiful Seal Point Siamese – and in 1965 Petra had eight puppies. They were all given to homes where they'd bring a lot of people pleasure, but we decided to keep the eighth puppy, Patch, and John Noakes looked after him. It was a tremendous shock when Patch died in 1971, and John's second Blue Peter dog was a Border Collie called Shep.

1971 marked the first Blue Peter Special. We were asked if we'd like to make a film with Princess Anne. The Princess had just become President of the Save the Children Fund and had agreed to appear in a film about the Fund's work in Kenya. Valerie Singleton was invited to join her, and that's how the Blue Peter Royal Safari began. It included a visit to a Kikuyu village and Tree Tops - the unique tree house in the middle of a game reserve where in 1952, Princess Anne's mother heard she had become Queen, and Valerie

Simon and Goldie joined Blue Peter together in **1978**.

and the Princess went big game spotting in Nairobi's National Park. There was underwater swimming, too; but the main purpose of the Safari was the visit to the Starehe Boys Centre that rescues orphans and gives them new lives.

1971 was also the year we planted a tree outside the TV Centre for the second millennium – the year 2000. Nearby we buried a box for the presenters of Blue Peter to dig up in the year 2000, and inside we put souvenirs of June 7th, 1971. A map showing the exact location of where the box is buried is kept in the vaults of the BBC's bank, so if you're watching Blue Peter in the year 2000 – don't forget to write to the Blue Peter office and remind them to dig up the box!

The Royal Safari was the start of the popular *Blue Peter Special Assignment* series, and Valerie Singleton left the twice-weekly programmes to make the series about famous Cities, Islands and People. Val's place was taken by a dancer called Lesley Judd, who made Blue Peter's first-ever "live" broadcast from the USA, when she flew on the inaugural flight of the British Airways Concorde from London to Washington. The flight, on 24th May, 1976, covered a distance of 3,800 miles in three hours fifty-two minutes.

In 1979, Lesley decided she wanted to spend more time at home to nurse her husband, who had Multiple Sclerosis, and actress Tina Heath joined the team – but not for long! In Spring 1980, Tina announced she was expecting a baby – and the baby made Blue Peter history *before* she was born, because we showed Ultra Scan pictures of her moving inside Tina, and eight million viewers heard her heart beating through an electronic stethescope. Jemma was born on 22nd September, 1980, and has taken part in lots of programmes.

By now Peter Purves was trying his hand as a sports reporter, compering *Stopwatch* and the darts championships, and his place had been taken by farmer's son, Simon Groom. Simon joined Blue Peter with a seven-week old golden retriever puppy called Goldie by Blue Peter viewers, who is one of the programme's best-loved pets. During the attempted destruction of Cambodia by Pol Pot, and the starving to death of millions of men, women and children, it was Simon who became the first British Reporter allowed into the capital, Phnom-Penh, in November 1979, during the first-ever Great Blue Peter Bring & Buy Sale.

When John Noakes decided he'd fulfil his life's ambition and sail round the world, he handed over to another Christopher. Chris Wenner was an actor and he returned to the theatre in the summer of 1980, but not before he'd presented nine Blue Peter viewers to Her Majesty the Queen. They were the winners of our International Year of the Child Flower Picture Competition, and we filmed them meeting the Queen in Westminster Cathedral. So Sarah, who'd joined Blue Peter when Tina had her baby, and Simon teamed up with the programme's second Peter – Peter Duncan.

Acting is in Sarah's blood – both her parents are in the theatre – and she always said she'd return to the stage after her Blue Peter presenting. It was a lucky chance for the programme that Janet from *Jigsaw* was free to step into her shoes. So now the famous three are Simon, Peter and Janet.

One of the very nicest things about being 25-years old is that today's presenters are all ex-Blue Peter viewers! And who knows, a few years from now it might be *you* sitting in our studio at Television Centre, waiting for the familiar signature tune to die away, and watching, hawk-eyed, for the red light to appear on the camera and the Floor Manager's signal before you say: "Hello .... and that was ...."

And whatever "it" is – you can bet your life it'll be an idea from a Blue Peter viewer!

▲ Tina was the first Blue Peter presenter to have a baby. Jemma was born in **1980**.

▲ Christopher Wenner presented Blue Peter Competition winners to Her Majesty the Queen in Westminster Cathedral.

Percy started gardening with us in **1974**. We built our greenhouse in **1981**. ▼

ALL THAT GLITTERS..

'. . . Ronde de jambe – plié – bend your knees, Sarah – and arabesque.'

The voice was Brian Shaw, once a great leading dancer, now the ballet master for the Royal Ballet at Covent Garden.

The place was not the Royal Opera House, but the Royal Ballet's rehearsal rooms which are not, as you might expect, somewhere in Covent Garden, but five miles away in a suburb called Barons Court. The occasion was a morning class with David Wall, Jennifer Penney, Anthony Dowell and about twenty other members of the Royal Ballet.

Everyone who works in a ballet company, from the Prima ballerina to the newest member of the corps de ballet, must do their exercises in class every day. A ballet dancer is an athlete as well as an artiste, and his or her body needs to be kept to the same standard of physical fitness as someone like Sebastian Coe or John MacEnroe. I realised how out of condition *I* was after about ten minutes, because I gave up ballet when I was fifteen, and although my mind remembered all the exercises, my body was suffering from a severe shock!

I travelled back to Covent Garden on the underground with three or four girls who were appearing in *Cinderella* that night. A dancer is often doing very exacting physical work for ten or twelve hours a day, building up to a peak which is like running a 4-minute mile for every performance. Their lives, and the lives of all the top dancers, would be a great deal easier without slogging out to Barons Court every day for a class or a rehearsal.

The problem is space. The Royal Opera House, built in 1858, is one of the most beautiful theatres in the world, but back-stage the conditions are appalling. If it had been a factory, the law would have compelled them to close down years ago. The trouble is that the Royal Opera House is the home of not just the Royal Ballet, but the Royal Opera as well. Ballet and Opera need huge orchestras, vast wardrobes, corps de ballet, choruses, enormous sets and an echoing amount of space. They change the programme every night so that the storage space needed for scenery, costumes and props makes the mind boggle. The stage is always occupied by technicians, taking down or putting up scenery and adjusting the lighting.

Rehearsals for dancers and singers take place at Barons Court and in dozens of different

This isn't the Royal Opera House – the rehearsal rooms are 5 miles away.

The daily journeys waste dancers' valuable time.

The space needed to paint the scenery is colossal.

There's shortage of space for dressing rooms and costumes, too.

halls throughout London. I watched the Royal Opera House Orchestra rehearsing in the Crush Bar, which is a beautiful place for a drink in the interval, but not too good for the double basses and the percussion who had to crane round pillars to get a glimpse of the conductor.

If your idea of dressing rooms is based on scenes in Hollywood musical films with a beautiful suite of elegantly furnished rooms banked by bouquets of flowers, you're in for a shock if you visit the dressing rooms used by the world's greatest singers and dancers at Covent Garden. Not that they don't get their fair share of flowers from their fans, but they haven't got room for them in their dressing rooms, which have cracked wash basins and threadbare carpets, with hardly the space to swing a cat; and yet they have to walk onto the stage like glittering stars.

David Drew is one of those glittering stars and the night I went to visit him in his tiny dressing room he was beginning his 2-hour

All the props, for the Operas, as well as the Ballets, have to be stored in an overcrowded room in a basement under the street!

I checked that David's garters were straight before his entrance.

The Royal Ballet uses thousands of pairs of shoes every year.

transformation from a pleasant young man with a moustache into a haughty, over-dressed and ridiculous Ugly Sister in *Cinderella*.

David told me as he slapped on the grease paint, that he hoped that things would gradually get better for the dancers and singers. 'Not just for our sake, but for the people who come to see us, because we should be able to look better and perform better when we aren't wearing ourselves out fighting these conditions.'

There are plans to build a rehearsal room block and a costume and scenery store right next to the Opera House, so that eventually everything will be under one roof.

'It's going to cost a lot of money, though,' David told me. 'I hope they'll have enough to get it finished before my dancing days are over!' He started to stick on a turned-up nose. 'Do you know that more people go to the ballet in the course of a year than go to watch football? Pass me that wig, will you, dearie.'

I noticed that not only was David's face changing, but his whole being was gradually turning into an ugly sister.

'If all the people who enjoy ballet gave us 50p each for the new building, we'd be on velvet, dear. Do me up at the back – there's a love. That's right, now the beads and the garters.' He pursed his lips and looked into the mirror. 'Every inch a lady?' he asked. I lifted his skirt to check his garters were straight. 'Saucy monkey!' he said, and swept out of the room.

Half an hour later I was sitting in the stalls of the most opulent and glittering theatre in London watching David's brilliantly funny portrayal of the ugly sister in *Cinderella*. The ordinary young man with a moustache seemed as remote as the tiny, tatty dressing room he would go back to and take off the dress and the make-up and become David Drew again. I wished I could be like the Fairy Godmother and wave my wand to raise the new rehearsal block. But they don't really need magic – just a huge pile of 50p pieces.

DRESSING UP

WHETHER you're dressing up for a play or a fancy dress parade, or simply want to try out a new hairstyle, a wig like these could transform your appearance. Ready-made wigs can be expensive, but you can go punk, dizzy blonde, or bright ginger for only a few pence – and even Goldie found Simon hard to recognise!

THE BASE for all the wigs is a plastic mesh fruit or vegetable bag. (The larger the mesh, the easier it is to thread the wool or string through). The bag should be big enough to fix over your head and cover your face a little way down. Don't worry if it comes down too far because the spare bit can be tucked up inside the wig.

Woolly wigs

1 Try to use a thick, chunky type of wool, (If you're using a thinner wool use two strands at a time.) Cut off 10-12 cm lengths – not all exactly even. The wig looks better if it's slightly shaggy and uneven.

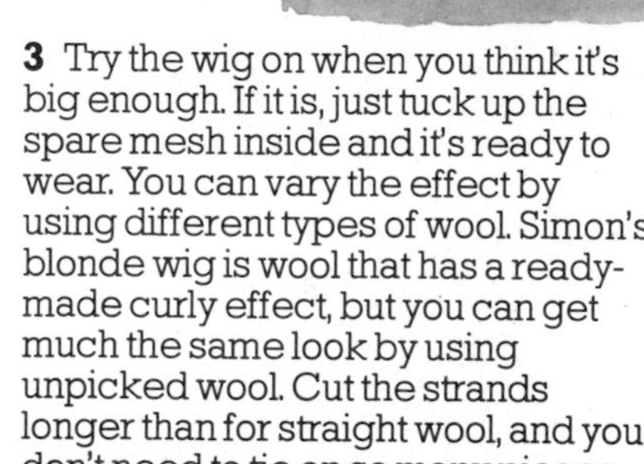

2 Put one hand inside the bag fairly near the top and spread out the mesh. Thread a strand of wool in one hole and out of the next and tie the ends of the wool over the knobbly part where the mesh is joined. Continue to tie on the strands, working evenly downwards to cover all the mesh.

3 Try the wig on when you think it's big enough. If it is, just tuck up the spare mesh inside and it's ready to wear. You can vary the effect by using different types of wool. Simon's blonde wig is wool that has a ready-made curly effect, but you can get much the same look by using unpicked wool. Cut the strands longer than for straight wool, and you don't need to tie on so many pieces as the length covers up the gaps.

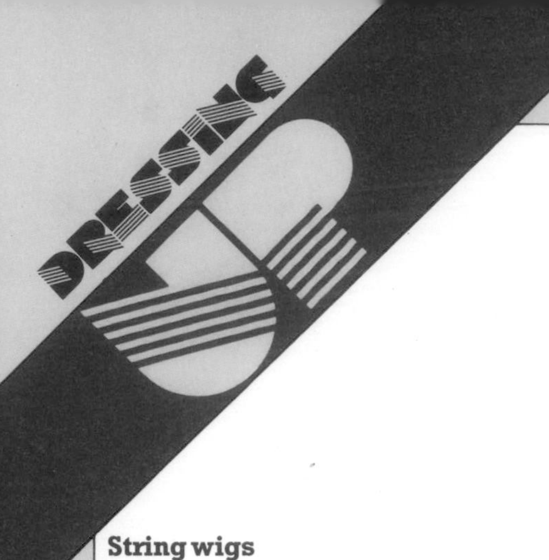

2 As you work on the wig you'll find the string fluffs out even more, giving a hairy look. Any ends that don't fluff out can be opened up with your fingers. The wig can be left its natural blonde colour or dyed. Use a cold-water dye according to the instructions on the tin – half a tin should be enough.

String wigs
1 For a punk look, cut off 10 cm lengths of sisal string, separate the strands and tie on the string just like the wool. Because the ends fray, it's easier to fold the strand and push the folded part through the mesh. Open it out before tying in place.

P.S. You can make dolls' wigs using the same method. The wig will fit your doll better if you thread thin elastic round the lower edge, tying the ends to fit the head. Pull the wool strands down to cover any elastic that shows.

CHIN FACES

DRESSING UP

THE three faces at the bottom of the previous page, take the prize for our spookiest experience of the year! Rebecca Patterson and her cousins, Joanna and Harriet Amos, had the idea during the holidays. Harriet was chatting to the others lying on the bed with her head hanging down. "We thought her chin would look just like a nose if we painted two eyes above it," explained Rebecca. So they experimented and came up with Chin Faces!

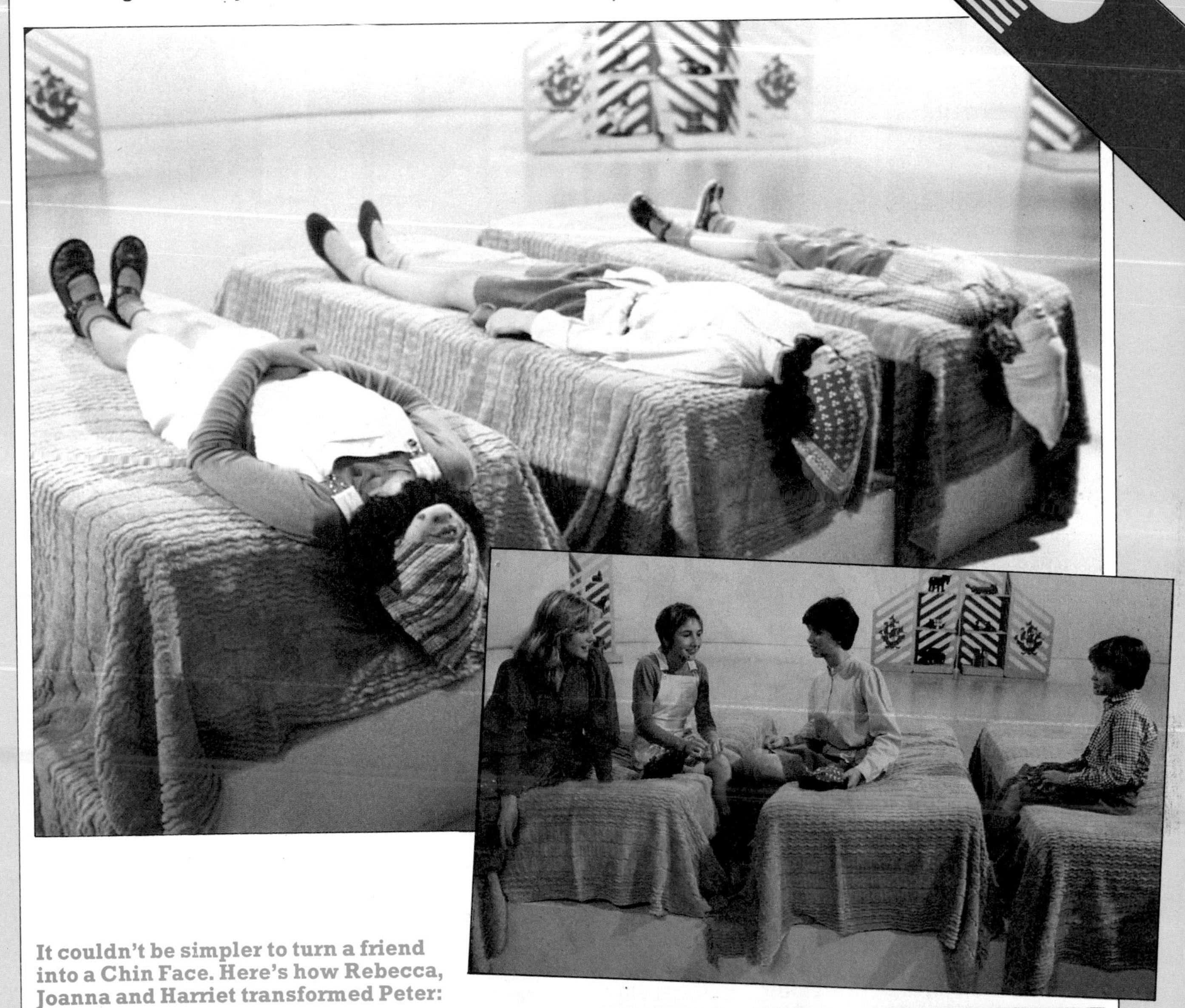

It couldn't be simpler to turn a friend into a Chin Face. Here's how Rebecca, Joanna and Harriet transformed Peter:

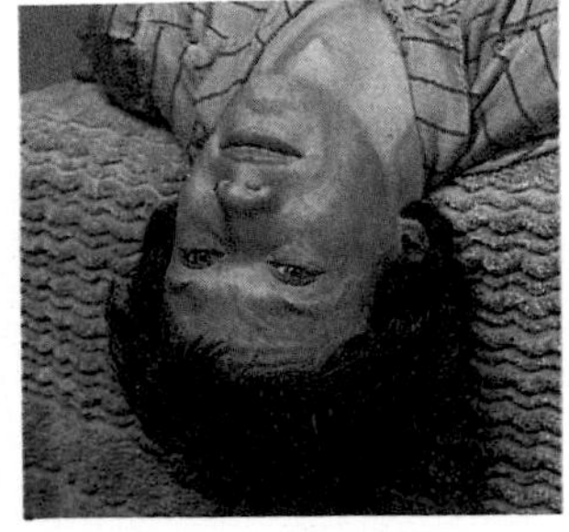

1 Lie back on a bed or sofa and hang your head over the edge.

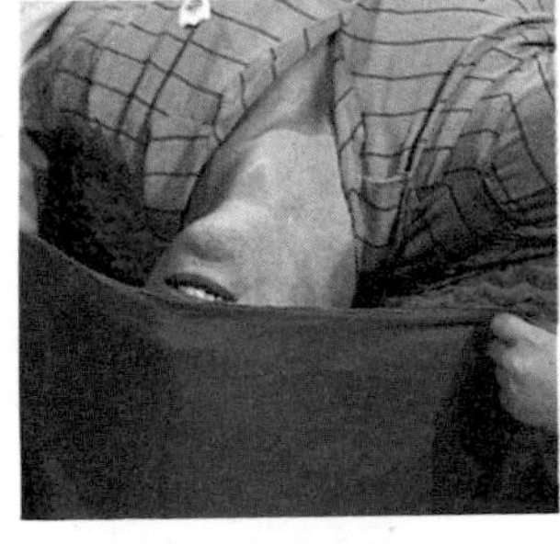

2 Hold a piece of material over your face, covering it from your nose to the top of your head.

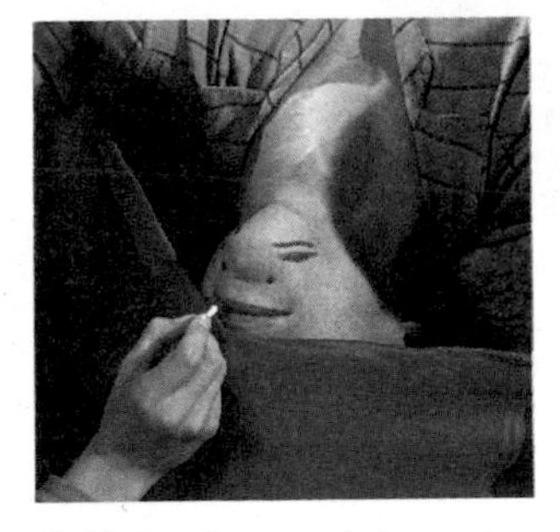

3 Using face paints, get a friend to draw eyes and two nostrils on your upside-down chin.

4 Bits of wool make effective "hair." When you start to move your chin and talk, the effect is hilarious!

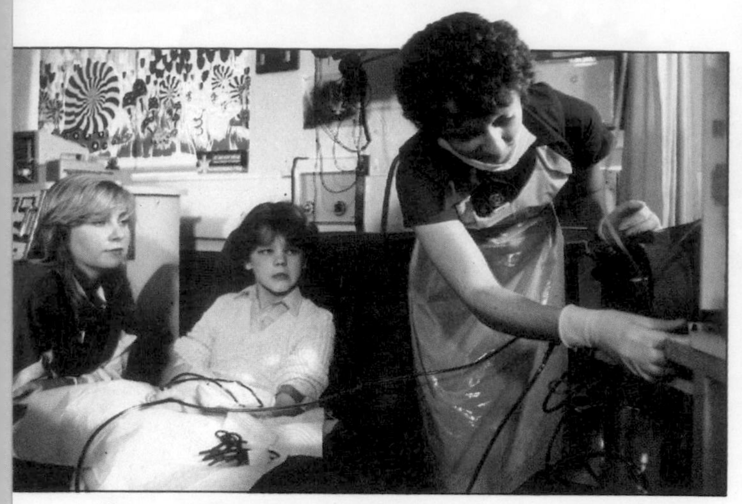

13-year old Tracy Mountford's life was saved at East Birmingham Hospital after she'd collapsed unconscious with sudden kidney failure.

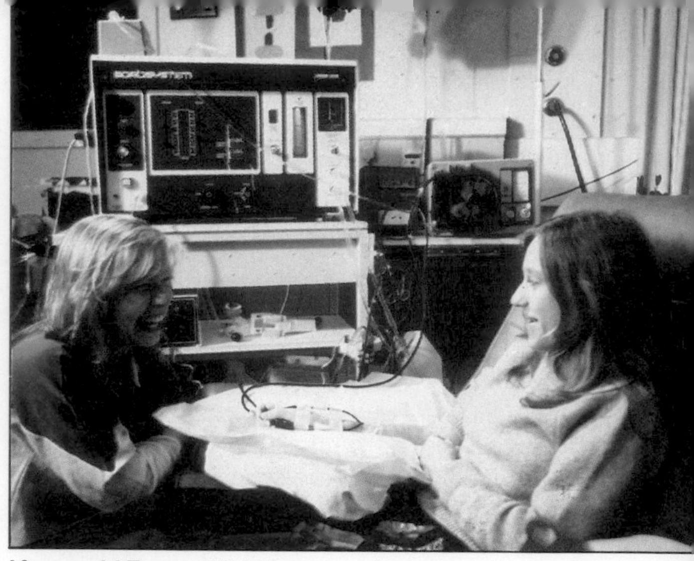

16-year old Tracey Whitehouse made such good progress, she's now out of hospital and dialysing at home.

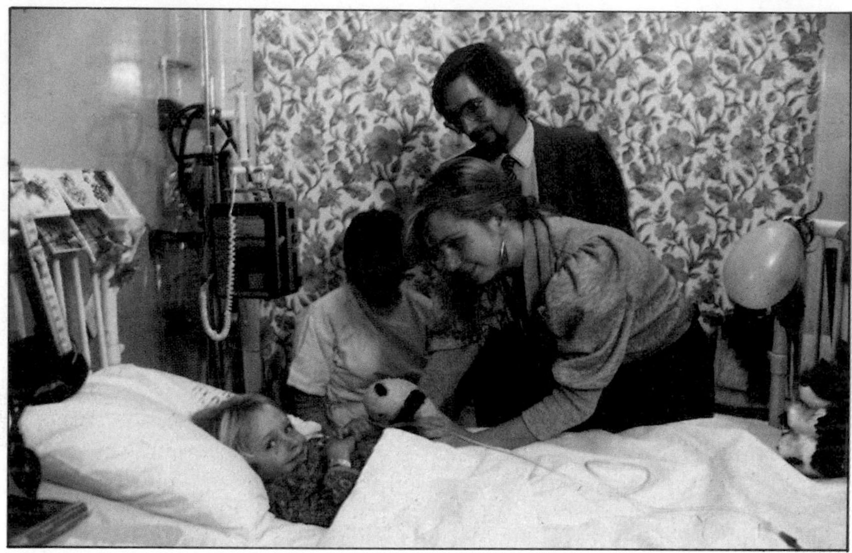

Above: Three-year old Jessie Baxter was rushed to hospital with acute kidney failure. Because she received treatment *fast*, her life was saved and now her kidneys are better.

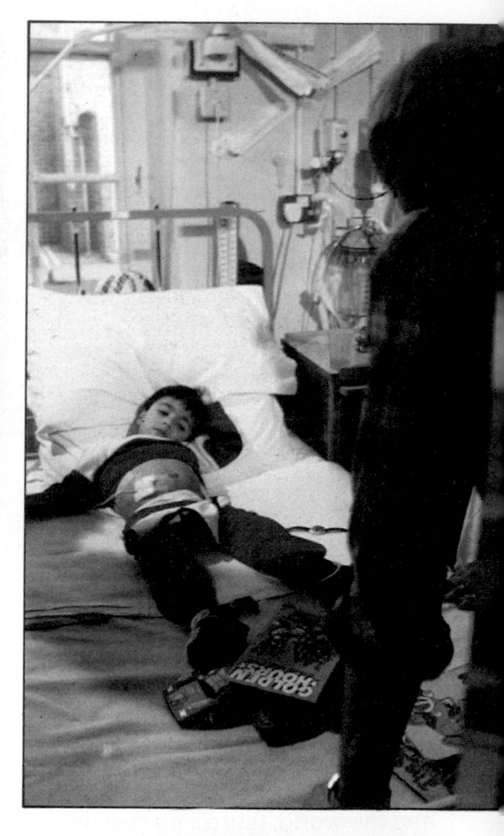

Right: Seven-year old Michelle was dialysing at Southmead General Hospital at Bristol using the CAPD method. There's a membrane or special piece of skin inside you that can act just like a kidney. To use it you need a plastic tube inserted through your stomach to let in the special dialysis fluid. Just as with an artificial kidney, this draws all the impurities from the blood – but this time through the skin that's *inside* the patient's tummy.

Left: Eleven-month old Andrew Spiers has regular check-ups at Great Ormond Street. He was born with kidney failure and hopes to have a transplant when he's 10 years old.

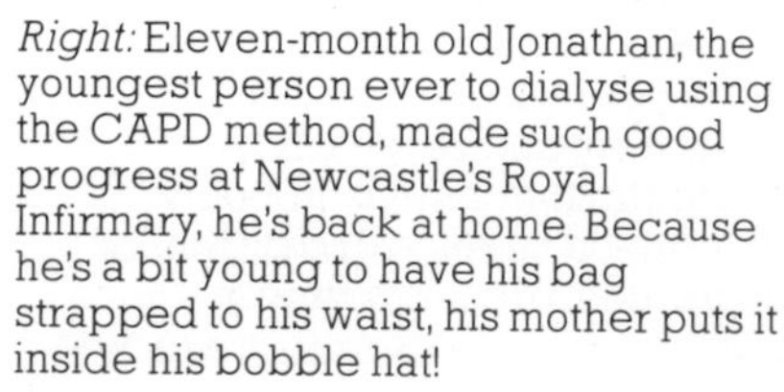

Right: Eleven-month old Jonathan, the youngest person ever to dialyse using the CAPD method, made such good progress at Newcastle's Royal Infirmary, he's back at home. Because he's a bit young to have his bag strapped to his waist, his mother puts it inside his bobble hat!

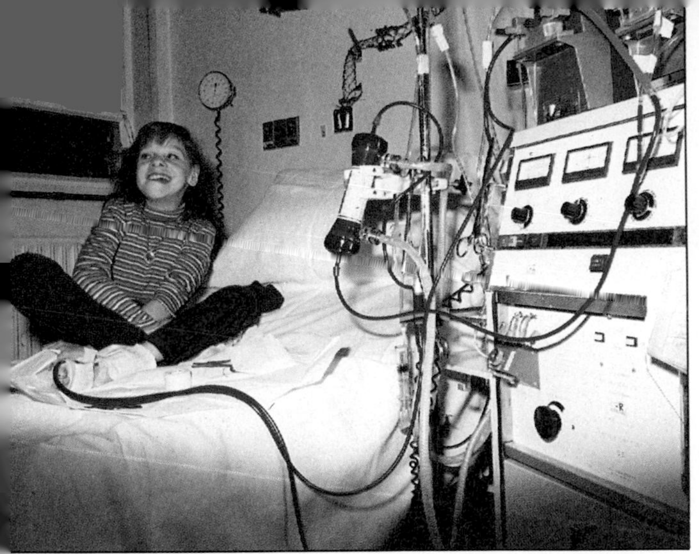

Although children can spend as long as 7 hours a day, 3 days a week, being wired up to dialysis machines like this, we were all impressed by their courage and cheerfulness.

People who are lucky enough to get a place in the special Children's Kidney Units can't go to school, but they have all their lessons in their hospitals – like this group I met at Bristol.

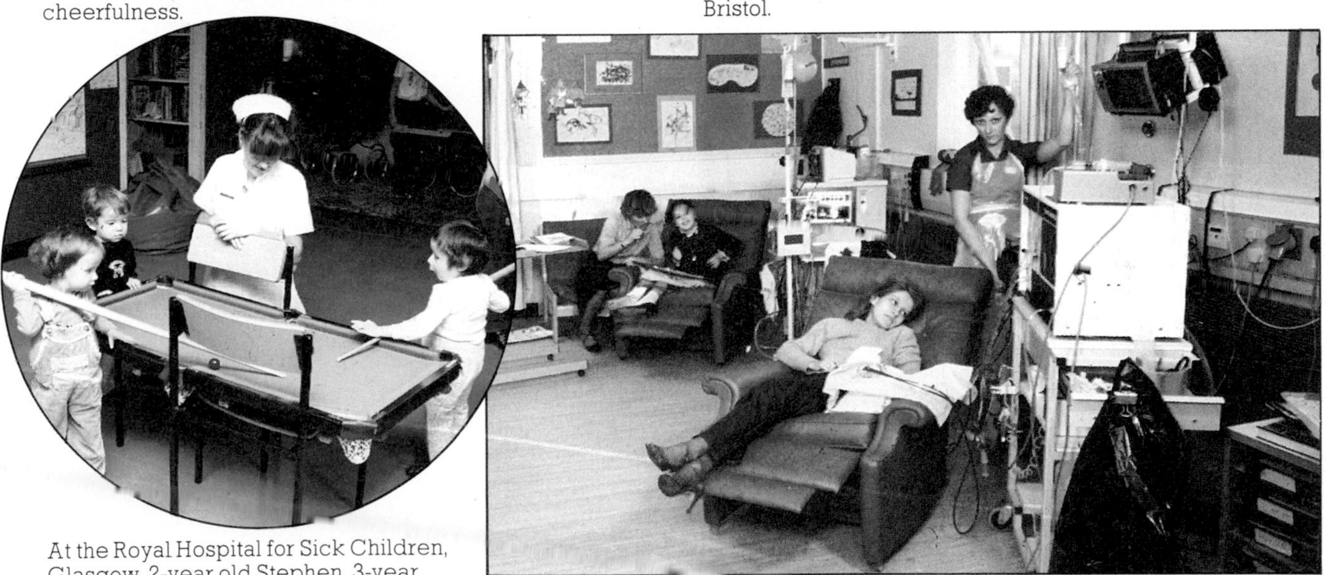

At the Royal Hospital for Sick Children, Glasgow, 2-year old Stephen, 3-year old Kevin and 6-year old John have lots of time to play with the nurses in between their dialysis sessions.

You can carry on with your homework or read a book or a comic to while away the hours while you're dialysing, but the whole process leaves you very weak and listless.

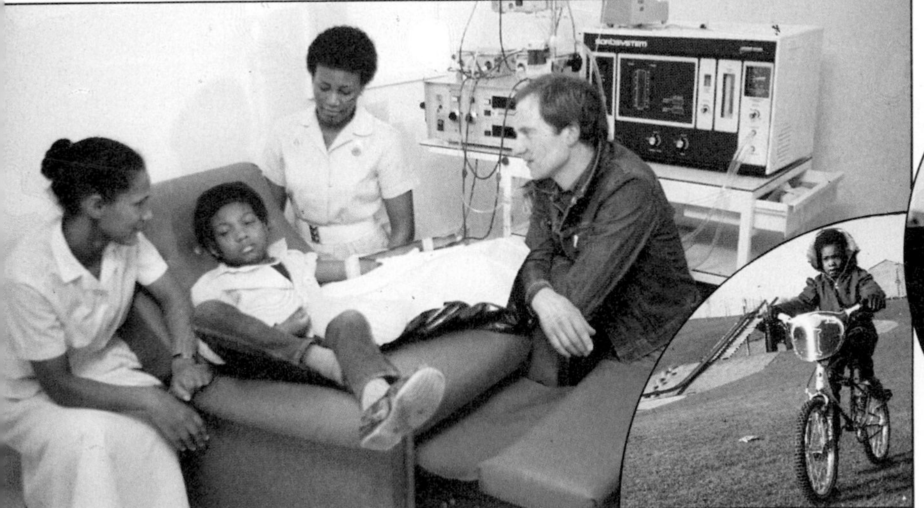

Above: One of our best bits of Treasure Hunt news was hearing that Gareth made such good progress in hospital he was allowed to dialyse at home. A room has been set aside especially for his equipment.
Inset: Three weeks later Gareth was well enough to pick up the threads of normal life. He still has to watch his intake of fluid very carefully, but he's making remarkable progress.

Dr. Winterborn, in charge of the Children's Renal Unit at the East Birmingham Hospital, made a magnificent gesture in aid of our Appeal – he shaved off his moustache and put it up for auction.

The Soest and Körbecke Brownies helped to pack treasure collected by readers of *Sixth Sense*, the British Forces newspaper in Germany.

A gift of knitted teddy bears from Mrs. Edith Kershaw of Oldham.

Roadline's massive container lorries provided free delivery of your parcels to the Treasure Hunt Depot. Scottish Parcels and Northern Ireland Carriers helped, too.

First in the free delivery chain came Britain's 1100 ambulance stations. They acted as collection points for viewers' parcels and delivered them to their nearest Roadline Branches.

Above: Collectors' items like these poured into our Depot. This 19th century gold and diamond brooch raised £420 at our Treasure Hunt Auction.

Right: By the spring of 1983, five million parcels had reached The Depot!

Chris Hawkings and his team from Phillips gave us expert advice on our Collectors' items.

Depot Manager, Arthur Randall, kept amazingly cheerful in spite of his mammouth sorting task.

I delivered my Mum's treasure to Bromley Ambulance Station.

Our first Collectors' Item Auction at Phillips created a record for a Blue Peter Sale – we raised £77,800! Sitting next to Sarah is Amanda Dutton, winner of our Mystery Object competition – the musical Christmas tree rotator.

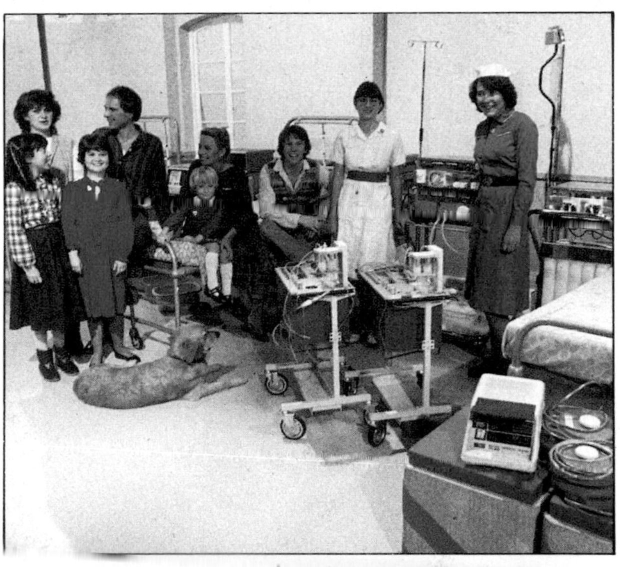

By January 1st we'd reached our target of 500,000 parcels. Jessie Baxter, Sharon Bassingthwaite, Clare Corps and Rachel Pryce, who'd all made miraculous recoveries from their kidney diseases, joined us in the studio, together with Sister Maggie Randall and Staff Nurse Amanda Welch from Great Ormond Street. This is some of the equipment your treasure has provided.

STOP PRESS ✸ STOP PRESS ✸ STOP PRESS

Our Treasure Hunt has been our most successful non-Bring & Buy Sale Appeal in the history of theprogramme. So far, your Treasure has provided:

Badly needed equipment for twenty hospitals where children and babies are on dialysis.

The equipping of a ward at Great Ormond Street for children suffering from acute renal failure, plus the running costs for 3 years.

The running costs for the Holiday Centre at Sussex Beach for 1984.

Five-year grants to the Renal Social workers at hospitals where children are on dialysis – for special diets, transport etc.

Grants to hospitals whose consultants are members of the British Association of Paediatric Nephrologists.

OUT OF THIS WORLD!

What do the Prince and Princess of Wales, Sarah Greene and millions of other humanoids have in common? They've all cried over ET – the creature from Outer Space in the smash-hit film that's been seen by cinema-goers the world over!

The day the film had its Royal Premiere here in Britain, one of its human stars, seven-year old Drew Barrymore, made a flying visit to our studio, before her presentation to Prince Charles and Princess Diana. Drew, who plays the part of Gertie, one of the children who look after ET, is the third generation in a family of actors. Her grandfather, John Barrymore, was the famous Hollywood movie star, so acting's well and truly in Drew's blood! She made her first appearance in a commercial when she was 11 months old, and starred in a feature film when she was 3½.

I thought it might have been a bit weird with an Extra Terrestial creature for a co-star and Drew agreed: "It was a bit spooky at first, but as time went by I kinda got used to him."

Acting with ET was a spooky experience for Drew Barrymore who played the part of Gertie.

Drew didn't get the part of ET because of her family connections. She auditioned for ace director, Stephen Speilberg, for another film called Poltergeist. She wasn't successful, but Stephen Speilberg said: "She's exactly the person I want for the girl in ET."

There aren't many seven-year olds who've starred in one of Hollywood's top box office successes, but Drew's not at all spoilt by the publicity – or by earning a great deal of money. We thought she deserved her Blue Peter badge for her Extra Terrific achievement!

A Podling from Dark Crystal.

Fizzgig, with his three sets of teeth, is a glove puppet.

Our next encounter with creatures from another world was when the Blue Peter studio was taken over by SkekEkt – the Skeksis – a fearsome brute whose idea of a good meal is a revolting mixture of bugs, beetles, dead animals, decaying vegetables and rotten fruit – a family of gentle Podlings and a creature with a big mouth and three sets of ferocious teeth, called Fizzgig. They were characters from the film The Dark Crystal, a tale of good versus evil, and they're the creation of Jim Henson, the man who invented the Muppets.

The Skeksis, the Podlings and Fizzgig are all puppets, but they're animated in different ways. SkekEkt was worked by radio and remote control, and he actually had a puppeteer inside him, too. Fizzgig was a glove puppet, and the Podlings were also animated by hand. For filming, the puppeteers had the exhausting task of working standing up with their arms above their heads so that the Podlings were at the right level for the cameras. Even with the film being made in very short "takes", they had to work like this for up to twenty minutes at a time, which was a great strain on the wrists! Each puppeteer had a small TV screen to check his Podling was moving properly for the film cameras, and a very strange sight they looked when they demonstrated their Podling dance in the studio.

The puppeteers animated the Podlings head high, using small TV screens to check their movements were correct.

A fearsome Skeksis and his favourite food.

Unlike the famous Disney cartoons, where millions of drawings are used to make the characters come to life, the Dark Crystal animation was created entirely by the skill of the puppeteers. The basic technique is a simple one, but with expert hand movements, fabulous scenery, masks and costumes, and very clever electronics and camera work, the final effect really is Out of this World!

Prince Albert's Greyhound

What on earth do you give to someone very rich who seems to have everything they want? A hundred and forty-two years ago, Queen Victoria had this problem, and she came up with a brilliant idea for a Christmas present for her husband, Albert.

1 When Prince Albert was a boy, he lived in a castle in Germany – he was Prince Albert of Saxe-Coburg and Gotha. And for his fourteenth birthday, he was given a marvellous present – a beautiful black and white greyhound puppy.

2 Prince Albert was absolutely delighted and he called her "Eos" after a Greek goddess. He was a very serious boy who worked very hard at his lessons, and he worked hard training Eos, too, who was very good and clever.

3 When Prince Albert was a young man, and Eos was fully grown, she went with him everywhere. He ordered her a beautiful collar from France. It was made of silver, and it was inscribed with her owner's name – in French – "Le Prince Albert de Saxe Coburg et Gotha." Eos looked a truly royal dog in her handsome new collar.

4 When Prince Albert was twenty-one years old, a great change came to his life. He travelled to England to marry his cousin, Queen Victoria, and he arranged for Eos to come to England, too. Queen Victoria loved dogs, and she was delighted to welcome the new arrival. "Dear Eos," she always called her.

5 Soon the elegant black and white greyhound settled down with Dash, the spaniel, and Dandie, Laddie and Islay, who were all Queen Victoria's dogs, and who were all much-loved family pets.

6 One day Eos had a nasty adventure – she was shot accidentally by Prince Ferdinand, an uncle of the royal couple, on a shooting party at Windsor Great Park. Prince Albert was very angry, but Eos recovered quickly.

7 Soon Victoria and Albert had several small children – and Eos was devoted to them. Queen Victoria said: "She is a sweet creature – she plays so much with the children and is so full of tricks."

8 Queen Victoria's favourite artist was Edwin Landseer, the great animal painter. One day she had a marvellous idea – she asked Landseer to paint a picture of Eos for Prince Albert's Christmas present. Eos was to stand by her master's hat and gloves and stick, as if waiting to be taken for a walk. It was to be a great Christmas surprise!

9 One day the secret was almost discovered – Landseer said: "Great was the bustle, when a groom rode up on a horse, all in a lather, for the hat and gloves, as the Prince was going out and must not miss his hat." The groom produced it just in time!

10 Christmas Day came at last. Queen Victoria and Prince Albert and their children had a beautiful Christmas tree and their presents arranged on tables. Prince Albert had to draw back a curtain – and there was the picture of Eos, just as Queen Victoria had planned. Prince Albert was surprised and delighted.

11 This is the picture that Queen Victoria ordered for Prince Albert's Christmas present. Eos' glossy black coat looks splendid against the rich, red tablecloth, and the hat and gloves that nearly spoiled the surprise, are in the picture, too. It's a lovely painting of a beautiful dog – no wonder her master, Prince Albert, was thrilled to have it!

12 At last, when she was ten years old, Eos died. Prince Albert and Queen Victoria were both very sad and they had this monument made for Eos in the grounds of Windsor Castle, rather like our statue of Petra. But the picture of Eos when she was alive and well must have been Prince Albert's favourite souvenir of his faithful friend.

Another souvenir of Eos still exists – the beautiful silver collar Prince Albert had made for her. Compared with Goldie's collar it was very small – because greyhounds have slim necks. The remarkable padlock has a large "A" for Albert and a special sequence of movements triggers the lock. It was a rare and fascinating piece of history to hold in my hand!

GUIDE DOG PRINCE

Prince and John Bates took to each other the very first moment they met. Off duty in John's garden, Prince knows he can relax when his harness is taken off.

Good Guide Dogs never scrounge for titbits!

The day Prince became a fully-qualified pair of eyes for the blind was one of the proudest moments of my life! All those months of puppy walking, the tests with Derek Freeman, and the crucial final training at the Guide Dogs for the Blind Centre at Wokingham, had paid off. Who would have thought that the noisy, bouncy puppy that had caused such havoc in the Blue Peter studio would be capable of guiding a blind person through busy traffic, on and off buses, *and* spend day after day quietly keeping an eye on his owner in a big, national bank?

The Obstacle Test
Prince's trainer, Brian Moody, watched as I wore a blindfold and Prince led me around obstacles that would be a hazard to his blind owner. This was one of the most diffcult of all the exercises at the Training Centre at Wokingham.

This time last year the Guide Dogs for the Blind's Puppy Walking Manager – better known to you and me as our old friend Derek Freeman – had selected Prince to go on to his Advanced Training. If Prince's four weeks at Derek's Puppy Walking Centre at Tolgate had been like going to school – the move to Wokingham was rather like University. Prince's lessons became much more complicated – he had to learn not only how to circumnavigate tricky obstacles, but how to guide a human being past them, too. Day after day Prince would lead a trainer wearing a blindfold through a maze of scaffolding and road signs set up in the grounds of the Centre.

This enabled the trainer to learn more about Prince – he could sense through the harness how Prince was reacting to the responsibility of leading him unaided.

When we took Blue Peter film cameras to report on

John and Prince out for their first walk together. The dogs and their new owners spend 4 weeks at the Centre.

Prince is an adaptable dog. He has always settled down quickly in new surroundings. He's John's second guide dog – the first dog, Lonnie, has retired but still lives with the Bates family.

John does everything for Prince including giving him his daily meal of meat and biscuits. Every six months a trainer from the Wokingham Centre comes to see how Prince is getting on.

All Prince's puppy walking training stands him in good stead. Like all good Guide Dogs, he won't growl or snap when his food is touched.

With Prince as his "eyes", John's life is transformed. He works as a telephonist at his local bank.

John wipes Prince's muddy paws – Guide Dog owners like to feel their dogs depend on them.

Prince's progress, I had a go at wearing the blindfold. Up until now it had always been me telling Prince what to do – it was a strange feeling knowing that if he made the slightest mistake I'd knock my shins or my head on one of the obstacles. I tried to relax – I could feel which way Prince wanted me to go, through the harness – but it needed maximum concentration – from both of us!

For the final four weeks, the new blind owners come to the Centre to have their first meetings with their dogs and to train together. This is always a tense time. Although dogs and humans are matched very carefully together, unless there's a mutual bond of love and trust the relationship won't work. Would Prince like his new owner, I wondered? Would the new owner like Prince? All I could do was wait and see as I walked quietly into the room where the meeting was to take place.

What followed next brought a lump to my throat. Prince had been chosen for John Bates, a blind bank worker. As John stretched out his hand, Prince ran forward and licked it. 'There's Prince', I said, and John put his arms round Prince's neck.

'Oh, he's a lovely boy – aren't you a lovely boy, Prince!' Prince's tail was wagging furiously and he licked John's ears and nose.

'Oh yes – you're lovely!' said John. It was instant love!

SUPER GUY

A hairy Super Star died on 6 June, 1978. He wasn't as tall as Sarah, but he weighed more than Peter and I put together. Just like a film star, his death hit the headlines world wide in the press and on TV – but he wasn't human – he was a Gorilla!

Guy was born in French West Africa and came to London from the Paris Zoo in 1947 when he was one year old. He travelled in a small tea chest and because he was looked after by a man called Mr Fookes, and arrived on November the fifth, London Zoo decided to call him Guy.

He flourished at the zoo and grew to be a magnificent adult. But despite his massive strength – he could have broken a man's neck with a twist of one wrist – Guy was a truly gentle giant. He was known to catch sparrows who flew into his enclosure, and after holding them for a while, he'd release them unharmed.

Guy became a tremendous favourite with visitors and was very clever at cadging tit-bits from them. One of his tricks was to rub his stomach and wave his hands which encouraged people to throw food to him. But this, alas, was his undoing. He died from a heart attack following an operation for the removal of decaying teeth – a result of too many sweets given to him by visitors.

But Guy, who ranks with Jumbo the Elephant, Brumas the Polar Bear, and Chi-Chi the Giant Panda, as one of London Zoo's greatest stars, lives on. His skin was preserved by the taxidermy unit at the Natural History Museum and at London Zoo there's a less spooky, but just as realistic a replica of him outside the Chimp House. It's a giant bronze sculpture by our old friend, William Timyn, who created the bronze head of Petra that stands in front of Television Centre.

Guy was always Tim's top favourite model at the zoo. He'd made a small sculpture of him just before he died and I was curious to know what caused this fascination!

'He was very powerful and strong,' said Tim. 'And he was so dominant. I mean, if you were standing in front of his cage when you looked at him, you couldn't help feeling inferior.'

'It's all very well making a small model,' I said, 'but how on earth are you going to create a Gorilla five times larger than life?'

The answer was a pantograph! At the Morris-Singer Foundry at Basingstoke, Tim made a plaster cast of his small model of Guy, marked it in sections and then numbered it. These small sections were enlarged on the biggest three-dimensional pantograph machine I'd ever seen. A small wheel followed the contours of the sections and transferred the shape onto a much bigger disc that enlarged it five times. Each enlarged section was marked on to sheets of polyurethane foam, and when they were cut out, it was simple to build them together to recreate the larger-than-life contours of Guy's body and face. A framework of aluminium struts became his bones.

'I want to convey the power,' said Tim, as his assistant, Alma,

Tim's small plaster cast of Guy was marked in sections and numbered – and each small section was enlarged by a huge 3-dimensional pantograph.

The enlarged Guy with the original small model.

A layer of rubber was painted over the model of Guy's head. When it was removed, liquid wax was poured inside the rubber skin.

smoothed the rough edges off Guy's gi-normous arms. 'But his face and skin I shall mould myself. Come to my garage!'

It wasn't quite as weird as it sounds. Tim uses his north London garage as his studio and this is where he covered the angular slices of Guy's polyurethane head with thick layers of modelling clay.

'What's the most difficult part of his face?' I asked.

'The nose!' replied Tim. 'It's a very interesting shape – very broad – and the little bit in the middle where the two nostrils meet together – that was difficult to work out.'

To keep the modelling clay in shape, Tim covered it with resin – except for one small area on Guy's left leg, where he added his distinctive signature.

Then Guy had to be cut up all over again! Back at the foundry, a layer of rubber was painted over the model of Guy's head and carefully removed. Liquid wax was poured inside the rubber skin, and when the wax hardened, a layer of ceramic was poured all over the front and back of Guy's face. A ceramic shell was baked over it and it took twelve hours cooking in a huge oven to harden. By then, of course, the wax impression inside had melted, and then came the most tricky stage of all – to pour molten metal *inside* the shell.

I helped to position Guy's head firmly in a bed of sand. Meanwhile, the foundry furnace was heating the bronze, which is a mixture of copper, tin, zinc and lead, to 1200° Centigrade.

'Take care,' warned Tim as the molten bronze was being transferred from the furnace. 'One drop on your shoe will burn a hole right through!'

I stood well back as Janet poured the bronze right into Guy's head through a series of hollow rods. The knack is to keep the metal flowing evenly into the mould until it's full – rather like filling up a hot-water bottle. But if you hesitate and let any air bubbles get inside, the whole thing is ruined.

Because the heat was so intense, we had to wait a nailbiting three hours before we could scrape off the ceramic shell and see whether or not the casting was any good. Tim kept amazingly calm. But as Guy's face emerged, he became quite excited.

'Yes – you can see the eyes – the nostrils – it's very good – it's coming along nicely.'

Slowly but surely all the other parts of Guy were moulded and baked, and after a three-day welding session and a final treatment with acid to make it a glossy dark colour, the bronze Guy was completed.

But the final test was still to come! After a speedy journey along the M3 on the back of a

Guy was sprayed with acid to give him a dark glossy coat.

Tim gave Guy's face a final spit and polish before the journey to the zoo.

It's no joke manoeuvring ¾-ton of solid bronze!

lorry, which caused passing motorists to blink and rub their eyes, Guy reached his old home – London Zoo.

As he was being unloaded outside the Ape House, I spotted George Callard, the keeper who'd looked after the real Guy for over thirty years.

'What do you think, George?'

'It's very nice,' he replied. 'A good similarity.' High praise indeed! But the verdict wasn't unaminous. There was a huge kerfuffle coming from the chimps.

'The chimps don't like it at all,' said George. 'They may not come out tomorrow – they don't like change and they don't like strange things – but they'll get used to it in time.'

You may not believe this – but I could swear that one of Guy's beady little eyes gave me a wink. It was just as though he was saying 'Guy is dead – long live Guy!'

The bronze Guy looks truly magnificent – from every angle!

Guy caused quite a stir as he sped along the M3. When he reached the zoo and was winched into position, the verdict from the crowds was unanimous – Guy looked terrific! See what you think of Tim's masterpiece the next time you're near the Ape House.

UP, UP AND ...

There is nothing quite so unpromising as a deflated hot air balloon.

The first one I saw lay like a huge dead moth on the grass in the middle of an Oxfordshire field.

But the tranquility was soon shattered by a great, roaring noise as Alan Holes and Philip Prout directed their hot air blower into the mouth of the balloon. A small ripple ran across the surface of the nylon; the ripple became a bubble and the bubble began to swell until it occupied the whole sack, which began to rise into the air. The tiny basket, which was to be my cockpit, was revealed beneath the massive ball of nylon that was straining at the tethering ropes.

John Albury helped me aboard and I glanced nervously up at the tongues of flame as they roared into the open end of the balloon.

'You've nothing to worry about, Sarah. It's a lovely day – very little wind.'

...AWAY!

'I beg your pardon . . .'

'I said it's a very quiet day,' he yelled over the noise of the burners.

I tucked my hair into my crash helmet and gripped the sides of the basket. I felt a sudden lurch under my feet – another roar from the burner – and then, slowly and smoothly, the ground began to slip away. I was looking down on Alan and Philip – looking down on the whole field – looking down on the dinky cars speeding along the road. I was up – up – and away!

It was the most wonderful feeling. In between the bursts from the burner there was absolute silence. Flying up 'til now had always been connected with noise, and it is the noise that gives you the confidence of being driven through the air. But this was different. I felt completely calm as I watched the silent cows in the silent fields, and dipped over the silent churches in the silent model villages.

JANET JUMPS IN!

JANET ELLIS

Birthday	16th September
Birthplace	Kent
Height	5' 2½"/ 158 cm.
Colour of Hair	Dark Brown
Colour of Eyes	Green
Hobbies	Singing, dancing, cinema, sewing, collecting very small teddy bears
School & Training	7 schools! Then Central School of Speech & Drama, theatre and TV work including Dr. Who and Jigsaw.
Favourite Food	Seafood
Favourite Colour	Red
Favourite Music (classical)	Mendelssohn, Sibelius, Holst
Favourite Music (pop)	Paul McCartney, 10 C.C., Human League
Favourite Sport	Roller skating, tennis
Ambition	To sing with a pop group (amongst lots of others)
Likes	Funfairs, cats, rainbows
Dislikes	Broken telephones, rudeness

All about Janet

Photos of Janet on the trampoline appeared in nearly every newspaper the day she joined Blue Peter

One of my tests before I joined the programme was to demonstrate this inflatable robot.

Another part of my studio audition was making Christmas cards.

On Thursday, the 28th of April, pretty green-eyed Janet Ellis became the sixth girl and twelfth all-time presenter to join the Blue Peter team.

"I've been a Blue Peter fan all my life," said Janet at a Press Conference held in the Blue Peter garden in front of *Newsround* cameras and dozens of newspaper photographers. "Val and Chris Trace were my idols when I was 7 years old."

Janet has come a long way since those days. Her father was a soldier serving in Germany, so she moved around a lot as a child, attending seven schools in England and Germany before beginning her serious training as an actress at the Central School of Speech and Drama in London.

In 1977 she got her first Television job when she played Princess Grizelda in *Jackanory Playhouse*, and soon after that she was in *Dr. Who* playing another Princess. This time it was Princess Theeka in *The Bulls of Nimon* when Tom Baker was Dr. Who. Her biggest break was when Television Producer Clive Doig chose her to be the girl who brings sanity and order to the crazy world of Jig, Adrian, Biggun and the Omen in *Jigsaw*, which won the British Academy Award for the Best Children's Programme in 1980.

But it was at the beginning of this year that Janet heard a rumour that Sarah might be leaving Blue Peter to go back to acting. It was, at that time, a closely guarded secret which very few people shared.

"I thought – there's only one way to find out. I'll go and ask the Head of Children's programmes! He ought to know!"

Two weeks later she was attending an audition in the Blue Peter studio in front of Editor, Biddy Baxter.

"It was absolutely terrifying," she confessed after it was all over. "Although Biddy and all the crew were very nice and put me at my ease, I knew a lot of other famous people were being considered, and – well – there was a lot at stake."

The audition was a kind of mini-Blue Peter. Janet had to demonstrate a radio-controlled robot. "It didn't seem to pay much attention to the buttons I was pressing, but I got by."

"After that I had to interview one of the Blue Peter directors, who was pretending to be a microlight pilot. I remember asking how he learnt to fly an aeroplane which only had space for one person. As he wasn't the real pilot, he hadn't the foggiest idea!"

"I quite enjoyed making the Christmas card. I'd actually seen Val, Lesley and Sarah doing something very similar over the years, so I felt on pretty safe ground – although demonstrating a "make" on television is not as easy as it looks."

Biddy Baxter thinks that the trampoline is a very important test. "When you're trying to interview someone whilst you're bouncing up and down, it's impossible to follow a set plan – a bit of the real you is bound to slip out."

But the real Janet Ellis was visible throughout the audition. "Once I started, I just felt I'd come home. When you're doing something you've wanted to do all your life, I suppose you can't help but do it naturally."

"What's your ambition when you join the Blue Peter team?" she was asked by one of the reporters at the Press Conference. Janet drew herself up to her full 5'2". "To be the first Blue Peter girl to do a free-fall parachute drop," she said, without a second's hesitation.

It looks as though the Flying Falcons are about to sign on their shortest, prettiest, but perhaps the most determined, recruit!

On April 28th I joined the Blue Peter team!

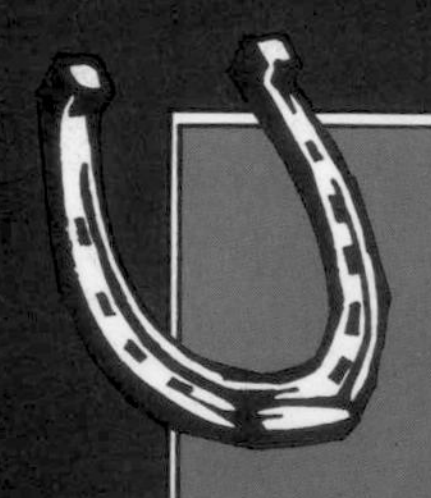

SEFTON THE

July 13, 1982, 10.45 a.m. The sun was shining and London was packed with tourists, all enjoying the sights that only London provide. The Changing of the Guard at Buckingham Palace was well underway and the Blues & Royals of the Household Cavalry had set out from Knightsbridge Barracks for their journey to mount the Queen's Lifeguard in Whitehall. It is one of the prides of the Household Cavalry to enter the Archway which divides Horseguards Parade from Whitehall as the clock above them chimes eleven. This means that they set out at precisely the same time each day and every stage of their journey is passed at exactly the same moment. This fact was known by the IRA murder gang who prepared the cruel nail bomb which, on that July morning, was to claim the lives of four troopers and seven horses.

Sefton's day begins at 5.30 am with "mucking out".

I was in Canada at the time on the summer filming expedition, but Biddy Baxter told me that the explosion was clearly heard 2 miles away in the Blue Peter office, and that everybody instinctively knew that something terrible had happened.

The great survivor of that dreadful day was a 19-year old horse called Sefton. He sustained 38 wounds from flying 10 and 15 cm nails, one of which pierced his jugular vein. His survival was a miracle, due to the brave troopers – some injured themselves – who helped to staunch the flow of blood with their bare hands, and the skill of Major Noel Canding, the Army vet. But everyone said that it was the cool bravery of Sefton himself which won the day.

Three months later Sefton was back on duty, and seven months after that I had the privilege of spending a day in the working life

WONDER HORSE

of that courageous horse.

Sefton's day begins very early, at 5.30 a.m., when he and the other 30 horses that share his stable in Hyde Park Barracks are "mucked out".

I drove through the deserted Kensington streets at 6.00 a.m. and turned into the very modern-looking tower block which is the barracks of the Household Cavalry in Knightsbridge. But once inside the stable I was plunged into a world of frantic activity. There were buckets clanging, horses neighing and stamping as hundreds of forks flung up piles of straw and horse dung.

"Come on lads – you should have finished by now," yelled out the Corporal of Horse. The countdown for the 11 o'clock guard mounting had begun – and they were already behind.

I found Sefton and Trooper Michael Pederson, who had been injured with Sefton on that fateful July morning. Michael, like Sefton, is now fit and back on duty. He threw me a dandy brush, and I immediately set to work on Sefton's flank whilst Michael dealt with the front end. There's an awful lot of horse to shine ready for the Queen's Lifeguard. As my brush passed over his gleaming black side, I could just make out the circles of the wounds where the merciless six-inch nails had pierced him. But today he was in great form with his ears cocked for the order for Michael to collect the oats and bran for his breakfast.

"Troop – Feed Away!" commanded the Corporal of Horse, and Sefton needed no second telling.

The next job was to whiten Sefton's "socks", and the man who told me what to do was Corporal of Horse Brian Lampard. He was the man who should have ridden Sefton on 13th July, but because of illness had to stand down. Brian gave me a piece of chalk, and after assuring me that Sefton had never kicked anyone in his life, left me to get on with it.

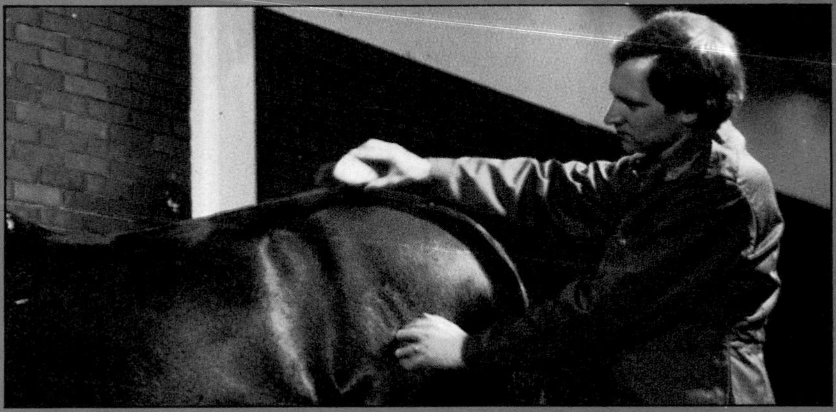

Sefton's coat has to shine as brilliantly as his rider's helmet.

Even his white socks have to be touched up with chalk.

"Who gave you orders to dismount, lad?" yelled Corporal Burns.

I was interested to see the kind of training involved in being a member of the Household Cavalry. The regiment have been charged with guarding the Sovereign's life since 1660. There is a huge indoor riding school at Knightsbridge, and here the recruits are put through their paces by Staff Corporal Burns on a gruelling 22-week course. If you've ever ridden a horse before, you are told to forget it and begin again "the cavalry way", and the cavalry learn to ride *without* stirrups. I stood by my horse, a bay called *Crusader*, and waited for the order to mount. There was no mounting block, no one to give you a leg up, and no stirrup to put your foot in.

"Come on, you should be up there by now," bellowed Corporal Burns. "Trot on – backs straight – hands like a surgeon, knees like a vice. This is not a death march – trot on!"

The jumps were a new experience for me, and for the rest of the lads, but Corporal Burns had no mercy. The trooper who went immediately before me fell off half way down the course, but there was no rush to pick him up.

"Who gave you orders to dismount, lad? Get back up there!" was the sympathetic message from the Staff Corporal.

The dazzling breast-plates, gleaming boots, and the rest of the magnificent uniform of the Household Cavalry are prepared the day before, which is not surprising as it takes up to five hours to get their kit ready for inspection. That, of course, does not include the horses' equipment, which takes another 2 hours, and the horse itself, which takes a further hour. And woe betide the trooper who tries to cut corners.

Sefton's rider in the Queen's Lifeguard that day was Trooper Francis of the Blues & Royals. He was sitting bolt upright alongside the rest of the troop, looking, to my eyes, the epitome of gleaming military splendour. Each horse and trooper was inspected by the Troop Commander with a thoroughness which amazed me. Every buckle, every strap was examined, turned over and re-examined. Trooper Francis had left a fleck of polish on the *inside* of one of Sefton's buckles. The Troop Commander looked as though he had seen something indescribably filthy. "Polish left on the buckle," he said, disgustedly.

Corporal Christopher Orchard (who I later discovered was a Blue Peter badge winner for playing a Euphonium on the programme 11 years ago) raised his trumpet to his lips and blew, which heralded the "Queen's Colour" – the flag bearing the battle honours of the Blues & Royals. The Colour was saluted, the order given, and the troop moved off.

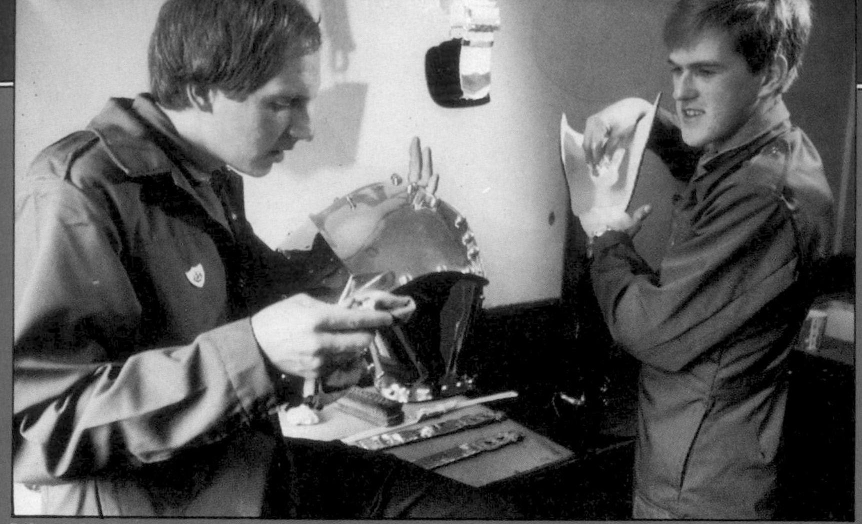
I thought that my brass looked really good until I saw what Trooper Francis called shiny.

It takes five hours to prepare the kit.

Trooper Francis and Sefton are ready for inspection.

The Troop Commander spotted a fleck of polish on the inside of a buckle.

A trumpet signals the arrival of the Queen's Colour.

The Horseguards journey from Kensington to Whitehall is timed to the second.

A few minutes later they passed the spot where the bomb went off just nine months ago. The men raised their swords to respect the memory of their comrades murdered by the IRA bomb.

I got out of my trooper's denims and joined the tourists to wait for the Blues & Royals to relieve the Lifeguards who where mounted in ranks on either side of the courtyard at Whitehall.

The clock chimed eleven, Corporal Orchard's trumpet rang out, and the Blues & Royals clattered over the cobblestones.

Sefton proudly took up his position and I watched tourists from all over the world jostling each other to take their photographs. I wondered how many realised that they were taking home not a record of a great British ceremony, but the portrait of a great British hero.

SEFTON'S INJURIES

These are some of the 38 wounds that Sefton suffered when the nail bomb exploded.

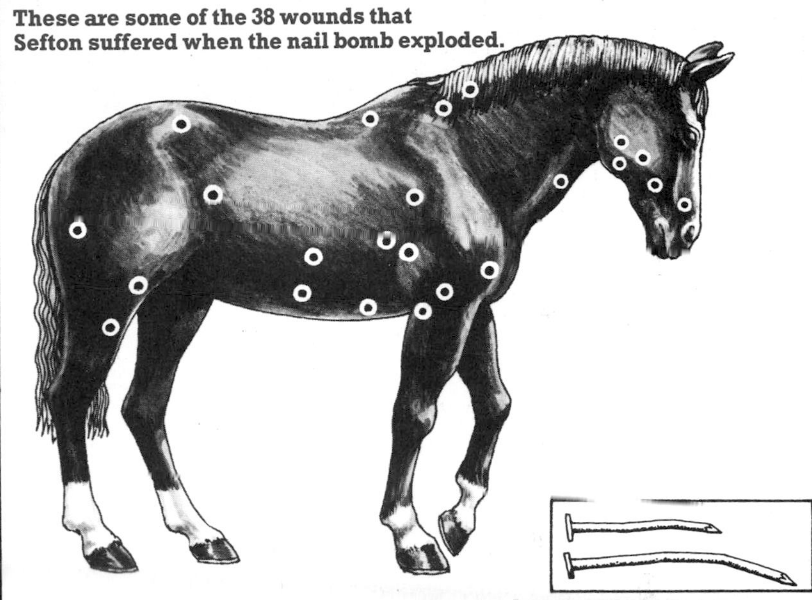

Hundreds of 10 and 15 cm nails were blasted into the air by the force of the bomb.

Every day they enter the courtyard as the clock strikes eleven.

I wonder how many of the tourists knew they were looking at a hero.

The Big Country

It seems odd, but as soon as you arrive in Canada you become aware of being in a country of enormous size. Coming from a little country like Britain where you can drive the 1400 kilometres from Land's End to John O'Groats in a single day, I felt knocked out by the realisation that it would take me 5 days to drive the 4,500 kilometres from the East to the West coast – and that is not the greatest distance between two points in Canada!

Everything about the place is enormous. Yonge Street, in Toronto, is the longest street in the world – 400 kilometres longer than the distance from Land's End to John O'Groats. Naturally, they have the tallest building in the world in Toronto, which, at 553 metres is not quite twice the height of the Eiffel Tower. And, of course, there is Niagara. Everything man-made suddenly seems puny and insignificant when you first see that magnificent horse-shoe with 3,000 tons of water roaring over it at every second, and the spray rising up to 150 metres – which is the height of our Post Office tower!

It is also a country of surprises. One day when we were in Quebec, the French-speaking part of Canada, we drove past a building with the sign 'Aerodium' at the front.

'Qu'est ce que c'est? What do they do in there?' I asked in my best French.

'Pas d'interêt à vous, je pense,' our guide replied. 'Eet ees just a place where peepul arr fly-ying.'

Pete who was nodding off in the back of the car was suddenly wide awake.

'Flying?' he said. 'Stop the car!'

Everything you've ever seen becomes small and insignificant after your first sight of the mighty Niagara Falls.

Pete had no idea what the guide meant, really, but we couldn't drive past a building where 'peepul arr fly-ying' without at least discovering how high – and where to?

As soon as we opened the door we were deafened by a roaring noise that made Niagara sound like a mountain stream. The huge, high room had a wire-mesh floor, and blasting through it was the most ferocious wind I have ever experienced.

Pete touched my shoulder and pointed to the ceiling. 'Peepul arr fly-ying,' he said.

He was right. Three figures in flying suits with arms and legs stretched out like frogs were riding on top of the air that was being blown up through the wire-mesh floor. We had walked into a free-fall parachutists' training centre – the world's first aerodium. Here it is possible to work on your free-fall technique without the expense of an aeroplane.

André, the man in charge, soon kitted us out with baggy flying suits, shin guards and crash helmets. Quebec French, as I was beginning to discover, was very unlike the French I learnt at school. It didn't have much in common with

This crazy place is the world's first aerodium where you can fly on jets of air which run up through the floor.

the French spoken in France, either. But the Quebecois are very friendly people, and unlike the French, they don't feel it is their duty to pull you up on every single mistake.

They turned the wind jet on to full blast and I began to walk across the wire-mesh floor. I felt the wind tugging against me and I started to lean onto the force of the jet. Suddenly, my legs left the ground – and I was airborne!

'Sarah, Sarah – pliez les jambes un peu!'

I remembered 'pliez' from my ballet lessons – 'pliez les jambes' – bend you knees!

It was the most incredible feeling – like being a tethered balloon, in reverse. One moment you were riding on air, but misjudge the wind direction for a second and you plummet to earth like a stone. I was glad the walls were so well padded.

If you played the word association game – when you're given a word and then you've got to say the next word that leaps into your mind – and the word was CANADA, what would you say?

Some might say 'Mountie', but nine people out of ten would plump for 'Lumberjack'. Timber has been one of the principal exports of Canada since its earliest days, and with it has grown up the tradition of toughness, which reflects the strength and the skill of the lumberjack. This is put to the test every year at a town called Sooke on Vancouver Island, when lumberjacks from all over Canada gather for 'All Sooke Day'. It's like the Highland Games, or the games held every year in the Lake District, except that every game in Sooke has got something to do with wood. Some are races with the axe and the saw – others use modern equipment like power-saws. Log rolling is a great favourite – and not all the competitors are men. The axe, of course, is the star – some competitors' axes cost as much as £200 each, and they are honed like razors, as Ian Moratti showed me when he skinned the hairs off my arm with the blade of the axe he was about to use in the underhand chop.

Ian took his place with the other competitors with their feet astride, standing on top of the log. The winner is the first one to cut through the wood between his feet.

The sound of the axes biting into the wood was almost drowned by the roars of the crowd as each section bellowed encouragement to their hero. The cheering was very important because all the lumberjacks are immensely strong and it needs inspiration to make one of them come out better than the rest.

But it's not all brute strength. The skill of driving the axe with hair's breadth accuracy to bring out perfect triangular wedges of timber is just as important – and the penalty for a mistake is chopping off your own toe!

'Come on, Ian!' I found myself yelling as his silver axe bit into the log which split apart seconds before the others.

But the skill that I had always admired the most was the speed climb. Lumberjacks need to shin up towering pines to lop off their branches before the tree is felled.

For the speed climb all you need is a pair of spurred boots, a rope and a belt . . . . .

Their tools, apart from the axe, are a pair of spurred climbing boots and a length of rope. For the competition there are no branches – just a 30-metre bare trunk and the fastest man to the top is the winner. The world record is an astonishing 27.8 seconds.

Steve Bartow, who is Sooke's champion climber, lent me his climbing boots and his rope, and took me to the foot of the pole.

'Put your hands as far round the tree as you can, Simon – that'll keep you straight. Now, just take a couple of steps up with your spurs – and throw your rope. That's great! Come on, Simon!'

The encouragement from this champion literally spurred me on, and I was up the first four metres very quickly.

'Very good, Simon. Keep your toes out so your spurs won't slip – you're doing real good!'

'One, two – throw up the rope. One, two – ' I panted to myself.

'Watch it now, Simon.'

One spur hadn't gone in deep enough and I began to slip, but luckily the rope held whilst I dug in again. I looked down over my shoulder and I could see Sarah and Steve looking surprisingly small at the foot of the tree.

'Maybe you should come down now, Simon,' called Steve. But I was on a high – and my mind had only one thought – the top of that 30-metre tree.

'One, two – throw your rope. One, two – throw your rope –'

'Simon! Steve's thinking you ought to come down, now.' That was Sarah with a slight note of anxiety in her voice.

'One, two – throw your rope. One, two, – suddenly my knees began to tremble – not so much from fear, but from sheer exhaustion. I looked at the yawning gap between me and the top, and with some slight gratification at the gap between me and the ground. I decided that perhaps the champ knew best, and began to make my descent, singing:

. . . . . and there's nothing between you and the top – apart from 30 metres of slippery trunk!

'I'm a lumberjack and I don't care . . . .'

They told me later that I got up 16 metres before I gave up which, when I looked back on it, scared the daylights out of me!

You make slits in the trunk, stick in a plank and climb on it.

Some of the tests call for the latest mechanical tools.

In a country as big as this, where over a third is covered by forest, the thing they dread most is a forest fire. If you remember that terrible bush-fire in Australia earlier this year, you will know the reason why. The conditions are very similar – vast open spaces of woodland at the end of a long, dry summer, which can make an area as big as the whole of France into a potential tinderbox.

The first problem when a fire breaks out is how to get to it, because there are hardly any roads through those remote forests. The only way in is by air, and the firemen use aeroplanes and helicopters as their fire engines. The firemen of Manning, in Alberta, had agreed to lay on a demonstration of aerial fire-fighting especially for Blue Peter cameras. We arrived just in time to see the crew racing across the tarmac towards their aeroplane.

'Good morning! We're from Blue Peter,' I said.

'Sorry man – we've got a real fire 30 kilometres away – but we'll try and send the chopper back for you.' The next minute they were gone, and we were alone in a silent, empty fire station.

This is as close as I ever want to be to a forest fire. The heat was unbelievable!

By mid-afternoon, when we were just beginning to think that we were stuck there for the day, a helicopter came clattering over the trees, and soon we were heading over the vast sea of pines towards a pall of smoke that was rising 10,000 metres into the air. Rick Arthur, our pilot, touched me on the shoulder and pointed down to a huge lake where we could see another helicopter scooping up water in a giant bucket which was dangling beneath him.

'When he comes up, he'll weigh another 2½ tons,' Rick told us. 'That's like as if 40 passengers had suddenly leapt on board.'

'What happens when he gets to the fire?' I asked.

'There's a remote-controlled flap at the bottom of the scoop – you just touch the lever, and suddenly you're 2½ tons lighter!'

We followed the helicopter towards the smoke which was now revealing a red heart of flame. It was as if the whole of Surrey was burning. We watched as he commenced a low run towards the smoke, disappear, and then emerge from the other side and head back towards the lake. The 2,500 litres of water was like emptying a plastic bucket onto a roaring bonfire.

Our helicopter dropped us at the base camp, which is a clearing in the forest, where the men live whilst they're fighting a fire. The camp gave me some idea of the scale of the operation. 360 men and women live there for weeks at a time, working for 20 hours a day and grabbing food and sleep when they can. I asked them if the fire ever caught up with the camp and forced them to move on. One of the tired men looked up from his cup of coffee and said, quietly: 'Five times in six days!"

A fire engine took me up to the front line where the fire was raging. It wasn't a helicopter this time, but the Nodwell. This is a huge caterpillar-tracked beast that carves its own swath through the forest, felling 30-metre trees like corn. It carries 14 tons of water in its tanks which the firemen use, not to fight the flaming trees, but to hose down the ground. Fire, especially in peaty soil, can continue smouldering underground for weeks. Then a fresh breeze will fan the embers and the fire storm is unleashed again. The main use of the Nodwell is to create fire breaks in the forest, leaving a clearing of bare ground, with nothing for the fire to feed on. As we approached the fire, the air became more and more acrid and difficult to breathe. I stood at the edge of the biggest bonfire I have ever seen, which would have stretched from London to the South coast. The heat was beyond belief. I managed to choke my way through the piece I had to say to the camera, when Ricky came dashing up to us.

'Come on, you guys. The wind's changing – and unless you want to end up barbecued, you'd better get out of here!'

We packed up the camera as fast as we could and made back for base camp. The helicopter took us soaring back over the fire as we headed for home.

I was tired, my throat hurt and my eyes were smarting. But as I flew in the direction of a shower and a change of clothes, my heart went out to Ricky and the crew. There wasn't going to be a shower and a cool, clean bed for them for quite a while.

The endless forests are broken up by rivers which for years have provided the transport for the timber to the sawmill. Melted snow from the Rocky mountains sends millions of gallons of icy water crashing through the steep canyons, which also provides Canadians with the sport of white water rafting.

Simon and I joined Herby, a very cool Canadian, on an inflatable raft for a death-defying trip down the Thompson river. The inflatable was very like one of our Blue Peter inshore rescue boats, and powered by an outboard motor.

Herby had been rafting down the Thompson for four years, and he knew every rock and every hazard like the back of his hand. He knew exactly when to put power on and when to let the river take over, and the current was running at 15 mph. We cut through the torrent and huge waves completely engulfed the raft, soaking us to the skin in icy water.

'That was a little one,' said Herby. 'The big one's coming up. This is the start of the Devil's Gorge – so I want you folks hanging on. Don't wave to anyone – just hang on, so we don't have to look for you in the water.'

Two minutes in that water and you'd either die from cold, or else you'd get swished to death.

By now we were freezing cold and soaked to the skin, and there was a bitter wind blowing up the canyon just to complete the fun. But it was the most wonderful, exhilerating, lunatic trip we've ever made, and I wouldn't have missed it for the world.

As we crashed through what Herby called 'the frog' in the middle of Devil's Gorge, Sarah pointed to a train chugging along a track between us and the mountainside. It was at least two miles long and it was being pulled by four locomotives.

Canada, I decided, is not only a big country – it's a country where they do things big!

"Don't wave to anyone," said Herby. "Just hang on – we don't want to have to look for anyone in the water!"

THE CASE OF THE BULLET TRAIN MYSTERY

Can you solve this case?
Six careless mistakes gave away the crook.
We spotted them – can you?

The train accelerated yet again as the world-renowned detective, former Police Superintendent McCann, bowed.

The serving lady bowed in reply and handed him two cups of coffee, and McCann offered one to his nephew, Bob, who watched through the window as Japan's countryside became a green blur.

Above his head, a speedometer informed him that the train was now travelling at 210 kilometres an hour. "These bullet trains are unbelievable," said Bob. "The name really suits them."

The globe-trotting private detective smiled. "Actually, that's a nickname invented by foreigners. The Japanese call them *Shinkansen*, which just means new trunk line."

"Bullet sounds better," said Bob. "They're certainly the fastest trains in the world."

The pair were standing in the buffet car on the bullet train that was speeding from Kyoto back to the capital of Japan, Tokyo. Both of them were inspecting the speedometer that is set in the wall for the curiosity of passengers.

"How are you liking Japan, then?" asked the great detective.

Bob shook his head in wonder. "I can't decide whether I like the old temples of Kyoto, or the new things – Tokyo is fascinating because it's all so new, but I'm sorry to leave a beautiful place like Kyoto."

"Yes. But I was glad to help the temple master there with his problem of the missing treasures. We can take a couple of days off before we get a flight back to London."

"When we get back, we must see that new show, the Hallam Big Band Extravaganza," remarked Bob.

The train slowed down decisively, and pulled into a station. The doors hissed open automatically, passengers rushed on and off at breakneck speed, and the train was moving again with scarcely a minute passed. "That's Japanese efficiency for you," said McCann.

"And yet the Japanese are so traditional and so polite. I think a Japanese would sooner die than wear shoes inside a house."

"It's not a country to wear smelly socks in," laughed McCann.

At that moment, McCann and Bob heard the very last sound they had expected: an English voice. What is more, it was an English voice calling McCann by name. "McCann! It is you!"

"Hello there," said McCann, to an immaculately dressed Englishman, who was wearing a dark suit and a bowler hat, looking strange in the throng of Japanese in the buffet.

"My name's Smithson-Smith," he explained. "You gave us remarkable help some years back in the case of the golden parrot."

"I remember," said McCann. "The problem of the sailor with the wooden leg." The two shook hands warmly. "What brings you to Japan, Mr Smithson-Smith?"

"Well, I'm head of a government group that is investigating the chances of making huge changes to improve British railways. It is my dream to establish a bullet train network in England."

"What a wonderful idea," said Bob.

Smithson-Smith smiled. "I think so – but a lot of people don't. In fact there are some people who are trying quite hard to stop us."

"Why?" asked Bob.

"People who make money from cars, who want to make sure that no one rides the trains any

more. So they have to buy cars instead."

Bob whistled.

Smithson-Smith said: "But look here, I must introduce you to my friend and helper, Mr Jolly."

A huge Englishman was shoving his way unceremoniously into the buffet car. "Hello vicar," he said cheerily. "Good to meet you all. That's me, Jolly by name, Jolly by nature."

He was wearing a hairy tweed jacked and a big, ginger moustache, and looked even more English than Smithson-Smith.

"And you are the official guide to Mr Smithson-Smith?" asked Bob.

"Not official, squire, not official," said Jolly. "Happened to run into this bod, and since I happen to know Japan rather better than the back of my hand, and since I'm also a great expert on railways, we sort of palled up – but look here, Smithson-Smith, old man, what about my coffee?"

But Smithson-Smith had suddenly turned a deathly shade of white. He was standing at the buffet counter, frenziedly tearing his hands through his pockets, desperately searching everywhere. "No," he said faintly. "No, it's not possible."

Bob froze. Something had plainly gone terribly wrong. But his uncle, McCann, snapped into action as fast as a speeding bullet train. "What is it?" he snapped.

"An envelope of paper. Plans, signed agreements with Japanese officials, a series of irreplaceable documents that would make my dream of a new dawn for British railways a little nearer reality. Gone! A year's study! Two weeks' travel throughout Japan – gone!"

"What is the envelope like?" asked Bob.

"Just a plain white envelope. I kept it in my pocket to have it close to me. I can't have dropped it. And I know I checked it when I got on the train in Kyoto."

Suddenly, without warning, McCann turned his back on the hapless Smithson-Smith. In normal circumstances this would have been appallingly rude behaviour. But Bob had the feeling that his uncle was up to something.

"I'll buy you some coffee, Mr Jolly," he said. He paid for the drink and again swapped bows with the waitress. "Actually, Mr Jolly, I'm surprised you don't drink Japanese tea, since you know the place so well."

"Oh yes, well, in Japanese homes I do, of course. Nothing I like more than to put my boots up on the table and have a good long natter over a pot of Japanese tea with my Japanese mates. But I've lived here for years, you see, I haven't seen England for ten years."

"You live in Kyoto?"

"Gosh no. I live in the historic centre of Tokyo, the really ancient part called the Ginza."

"And you're a train expert too, you say."

"Absolutely. The Japanese are frightfully fond of the bally bullet trains, that's why they invented the stupid name. But they're frightfully impressive machines, of course, top speed of a hundred miles an hour, you know."

"Amazing."

"Look here, chum," said Jolly. "What are we going to do about this fella-me-lad's envelope? Tear the train apart playing hunt the slipper? Where did you lose it, old man?"

"I – I lost it just before we stopped at the last station, I'm positive," said Mr Smithson-Smith. "Jolly and I had just been talking in the corridor."

"So we had. Well, I went off to stroll along the platform for five minutes, so I can't really help you."

"Haven't hidden it away in your pockets?" asked McCann with a disarming grin.

"Ha ha! Fine thief I'd make," laughed Jolly, and turned his pockets inside out to make a joke of his innocence. From one pocket, a ticket stub flew out and fluttered to the floor. Bob was surprised to see that it was a ticket for the Hallam Big Band Extravaganza.

"Well," said Jolly. "We're slowing down again now – looks like we're in Tokyo. I must go and collect my bag."

The train was slowing down rapidly, and was already pulling into Tokyo station.

"One minute Jolly – let's have the envelope first," rasped McCann.

"You're joking, aren't you, vicar?" said Jolly. At that moment, the train drew to a halt, the doors slid open and Jolly was through them in a trice, sprinting along the platform for the exit.

"After him, Bob!" cried McCann, and from a standing start, Bob took off like a bullet train.

For a moment it seemed that Jolly was too far ahead, but then at once he saw the tall, ginger-haired figure head and shoulders above most of the members of the Japanese crowd that was shuffling towards the way out.

Jolly turned his head and caught a glimpse of his sprinting pursuer – and that is where he made his mistake.

He spread his elbows wide, and tried to shove his way straight through the crowd, expecting the people to move away from his fiercely pushing bulk.

But it was not to be. The Japanese were annoyed by this ill-mannered, red-faced, pushing foreigner, and they pushed back crossly.

Bob used his head. Smiling and bowing to people on either side of him, he made his way through the dense crowd, who politely let him ease past them.

Jolly saw him approach, and pushed all the harder, but slowly, inevitably, the gap between them narrowed. Behind him, Bob could hear McCann and Smithson-Smith, but he knew that it was all down to him now.

Two people stood between himself and Jolly, and Jolly made a desperate lunge to move in the densely packed mass of people, but an old lady beside him refused to be pushed, and instead gave him a sharp clout with the corner of her suitcase.

Then Bob was on him, seizing his arm in a police arrest grip which McCann had taught him, turning his man round and leading him back to where McCann and Smithson-Smith stood.

His uncle flipped Jolly's jacket aside and there, tucked into the waistband of his trousers, was the missing envelope.

"Jolly!" gasped Smithson-Smith. "A traitor!"

"A spy, I think," said McCann. "Am I right?"

"So what if I am?" asked Jolly sulkily, all trace of his cheery good humour gone.

"Who do you work for?" asked McCann.

"I was hired by a secret group of car manufacturers to make sure that Smithson-Smith's findings never got back to England.

"We want to abolish all railways and force everybody to drive cars. I've never been to Japan before, but I shadowed Smithson-Smith, and then I fooled him. If it hadn't been for you, McCann, I'd have won."

"He didn't fool you for a minute," said Smithson-Smith in wonder. "How did you manage to see through this impostor?"

"He just happened," said McCann, "to make six very foolish mistakes."

"And it was those six mistakes," said Bob, "that were the six bullets that shot down the man who tried to rob the bullet train."

Did you spot the six mistakes?
Check your answers on page 76.

QUEEN FOR • A • DAY

Before I joined Blue Peter I was an actress. This isn't all that surprising because both my parents worked in the theatre before I was born, and my mother – Marjie Lawrence – still frequently appears on Television and in the London Theatre.

The real reason I wanted to act was an overwhelming desire to become someone else. I wanted to climb into the skin of another person, move as they moved, talk as they talked, and to dress in every detail like the person I was pretending to be.

Playing someone who really existed is, perhaps, the most exciting, because you can read all about the person, and by studying their paintings or photographs, bring the character alive again.

Since the earliest times, great Kings and Queens have been painted by the greatest artists of their time. The artists were no fools and they painted their monarchs to look wise and regal and beautiful – even if it wasn't always true. But at least they have left us a record of how they looked at their very best. This is true of one of the most brilliant, swaggering and regal figures in the history of England – Queen Elizabeth I.

The picture that actresses throughout the ages have used as their template when playing Elizabeth is of the Queen wearing what has become known as the 'Ditchley Dress', because she is standing in Ditchley in Oxfordshire, on the map on the floor. It was painted by a Belgian artist called Marcus Gheerherts in 1572.

Last year a young dress designer called Paul Sagers set out to reproduce the Ditchley dress in every detail, using the portrait as his guide. It took him 7 weeks to do it, and when it was completed, he lent it to me to wear on Blue Peter. And so very early one morning, with Paul's dress, and the skill of Judy Cain of the BBC Make-up Department, I began slowly to leave Sarah Greene behind and become – 'by God's grace – Her great and glorious Majesty Queen Elizabeth the First of England'.

8·00 My face is covered with white powder – high fashion for the Elizabethans –

8·15 – and my hair tucked beneath a gauze as Judy Cain produces a wig.

8·30 New imperious eyebrows are drawn above mine.

9·00 Although never seen, my underclothes were as authentic as my dress.

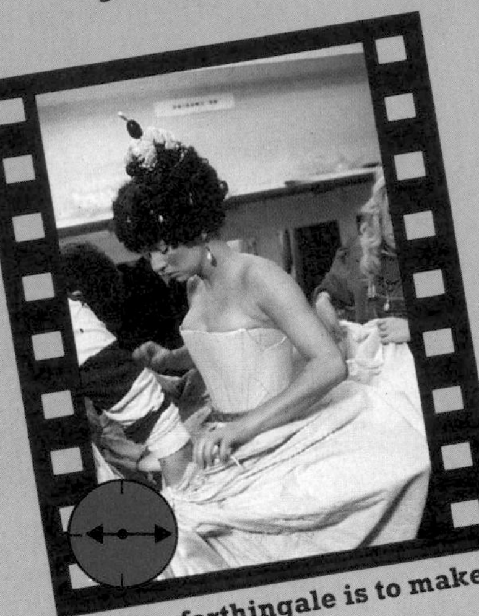

9·15 The farthingale is to make my dress stick out.

9·20 Pauline Korda laces me into the bodice.

9·30 The heaviest part of the dress is the large skirt.

9·40 My ruff – the most essential part of Elizabethan dress – came next.

10·00 Elizabethans would starch it using thin rods like pokers to keep it in shape.

10·30 Paul Sagers manoeuvres the large prongs that attach my veil to the dress.

10·40 Just a little arch on the eyebrow.

10·50 Framed as Queen Elizabeth

CRISPY MINCE PIES

Christmas wouldn't be Christmas without mince pies, and even if you're not brilliant at cooking, I'll guarantee you'll make a success of these. They're mince pies with a difference, because the crispy casing isn't pastry, it's bread! And because they're so quick and easy, you could make them as a last-minute present for a granny or grandad.

INGREDIENTS

12 slices of thin white bread
12 teaspoons of mincemeat
25 grams (3 oz) butter or margarine
25 grams (1 oz) fine, brown sugar.

METHOD

1 For the bases, cut out 12 circles from the bottom of the slices of bread using a pastry cutter, leaving enough bread at the top to cut out 12 smaller circles.

2 Melt the butter or margarine slowly over a low heat, and using a pastry brush, lightly cover both sides of the bases.

3 Put the bases into a baking tin and gently press into shape.

4 Put a level teaspoon of mincemeat into each of the bases.

5 Brush the small circles with the melted butter and dip the top sides into fine, brown sugar.

6 Put the tops over the mincemeat, sugar side up.

Cook in the centre of a hot oven for 12-15 minutes, Gas Mark 6, 400°F or 200°Celsius.

P.S. Crispy Mince Pies are best eaten shortly after cooking, and not stored in a tin!

Have you ever wondered what happens when you take the plug out of the bath – pull the lavatory chain – or empty the sink after a particularly greasy wash-up? And have you ever thought what would happen if one day it didn't all disappear to somewhere down below?

As I always seem to get the really attractive jobs on Blue Peter, it came as no surprise when I was asked to join Ben Nithsdale and his gang of flushers to penetrate the strange, echoey and smelly world of London's sewers.

On the day we showed my sewer film on the programme, Sarah announced that we were able to send our last cheque for £23,804.00 to Java for our Blue Peter Pipeline Appeal. Thanks to you, 150 villages now have fresh water "on tap" for the very first time, and thousands of lives of unborn children will have been saved because polluted water kills. If you had lived in London just over 100 years ago, you would have had the same problem. Thousands of people lived huddled together in slums. There were no lavatories with chains to pull, no sinks or

Even Royalty did not escape. Queen Victoria's husband died from typhoid because the River Thames was so polluted. Cartoons about the stinking Thames appeared in the newspapers . . .

. . . whilst the poor queued for water that was pumped straight out of the filthy river.

baths with plugs to empty the dirty water, because there were no drains below the streets to carry it away. But all that filthy water from washing clothes and people, the waste from the factories, the manure from hundreds of horses and from thousands of human beings still had to go somewhere. In most cities it went into rivers and streams, and in London it was sent straight back into the river Thames. The water companies drew it out again and sold it to Londoners, who drank it, believing it to be clean water.

They might as well have been drinking poison. It was the children who were particularly at risk from waterborne diseases like cholera, typhus and typhoid fever. One death in every three came from fever carried by polluted water, and 40,000 people died in London alone during two epidemics of cholera. The poor suffered the most, but Royalty did not escape. Prince Albert, Queen Victoria's husband died from typhoid fever, which comes from dirty water.

1858 was a long hot summer. The temperature soared to 94° Fahrenheit and the Thames, which was an open sewer, began to smell so

In the summer of 1858, the Thames smelt so bad that Parliament had to be suspended. They called it the Great Stink.

Today London has an efficient sewer system beneath its streets. I prepared to go down below with Ben Nithsdale.

badly that no one would sail on it. "It is filthy beyond the filthiness of the vilest plague spot in the East," wrote one contemporary commentator. Everyone was talking about "The Great Stink". Articles and cartoons began to appear in the London newspapers. The Stink pervaded the House of Commons, which stands on the bank of the River Thames, and the MPs had to abandon their sitting for the day.

This was the best thing that could have happened because it made the government take action. The man called on to save London from the Great Stink was Joseph Bazalgette. He was a civil engineer with plans for a complete reconstruction of the city's drains and sewers.

An army of men went to work to dig a huge network of tunnels beneath the streets. Gradually, London homes were built with water closets. At last there was a chain to pull!

But it is thanks to Joseph Bazalgette that the sewerage had somewhere to go and that death and disease through filthy water was conquered.

I was amazed to discover that Bazalgette's system is still in operation and is working just as well as the day it was opened, over a hundred years ago.

The underground world is as vast as the city above, with huge, echoing tunnels which correspond with wide, main roads and small caves running below the side streets. The whole of sewerland is mapped, because it is so enormous that a man could get lost and might never be seen again.

Ben Nithsdale kitted me out in overalls, a tin hat, great thigh boots, and a strong leather belt to pull me out in case I fell in the sewage. He heaved up a manhole cover in the middle of Green Park and we peered down into the murky depths.

Before we descended, Bob lowered a miner's lamp on a piece of rope to test for gas. If the lamp stayed lit, it was safe – but if the flame was snuffed out, it meant that deadly sewer gas was below and we would need breathing apparatus. The flame was still flickering when Ben hauled up the lamp two minutes later, so all was well. The stink came up and hit me as soon as I put my foot on the ladder, and it made me realise that if it hadn't been for Bazalgette, the whole of London would smell like this.

We climbed down about 4 metres, and then panned round our huge flushers' torches to reveal a long, brown, endless tunnel. It was 3

The roots of trees from Green Park penetrate the walls of the sewers and look like the Triffids.

Goldie was waiting for me when I emerged just outside Buckingham Palace!

metres wide with a small trickle of water running down the centre. I asked Ben how much deeper the water would be if it was raining hard above.

"In a storm, this tunnel is full to the roof," he said. The idea of being caught in a torrent of water in the endless dark was one that I quickly dismissed from my mind.

My torch lit up a strange triffid-like network of vegetation which appeared to be clinging to the roof of the cave.

"That is tree root infestation," said Bob. "If it gets too bad we would normally request the owner to remove the offending tree."

"And who's the owner of that particular tree?" I asked.

Bob's face remained, as always, impassive.

"The Queen," he said, and waded off into the dark.

I could hear a huge sound of rushing water ahead. We stepped over a 60 cm high sill into about 30 cm of swiftly moving water. I was glad of the chance to get my boots wet. I kept a wary eye open for rats – somewhere I had read that there were as many rats below the streets of London as there were Londoners above, but up to now there wasn't a whisker in sight.

Ben turned sharp right into a narrower tunnel and the noise of the torrent in that confined space reached Niagara proportions. I shone my light down a massive descending cascade of water and instinctively clung to the hand-rail on the wall of the tunnel. Bob's face remained expressionless in the glare of the torch light.

"If you fell over you would certainly die," he said.

"And it would not," I thought as I looked at the swirling, brown water thundering into the darkness, "be a lovely way to go."

It had been an interesting experience, but I can't say I was sorry when we stepped out into the sunshine again.

I was amazed to discover that we were only a stone's throw from Buckingham Palace. Had we been wandering through the royal drains, I wondered?

Surely not. But it is thanks to Joseph Bazalgette, that Prince Philip was saved from the risk of the same untimely death as poor Queen Victoria's husband. And I, for one, will be grateful every time I pull the chain to the man who saved us all from " the Great Stink."

Willo the Wisp

I'll never forget the day the Blue Peter studio was taken over by Willo & Co. Kenneth Williams, who invented all the voices, kept me and the whole of the camera crew in fits as he became Arthur, the cockney caterpillar, ratty old Evil Edna the witch who casts spells with her indoor aerial, and Mavis Cruet – the overweight fairy.

Nick Spargo, the artist who dreamed up Willo the Wisp, says there are between 2500 and 3000 different drawings in every film, so you can imagine how long it takes to make each one. But you'll find you can whip up your very own Arthur and Evil Edna quicker than Edna could turn you into a frog!

Materials needed to make Arthur

30 cm square of tan felt
Sewing thread to match tan felt
Scraps of coloured felt
Felt-tipped pens or crayons for features
Rubber solution glue
Stuffing (cotton wool or tissue)
Wire, two lengths of 40 cm and 15 cm
Round button or bead for nose
Table tennis ball
Black paper or thin card

For Evil Edna

Dark grey and light grey paper
Scraps of yellow, white and blue paper
Small buttons (3)
A small cardboard grocery packet
A black felt-tipped pen
A domed tap washer and wire

Arthur

1 Arthur's head is made from a table tennis ball. His nose is a round bead or button. Take a piece of wire about 40 cm long and bend in half, then thread the bead along to the middle and twist the ends together. To attach the nose to the head, make two holes in the table tennis ball as shown (get an adult to help with this). Thread the wire through the centre hole and out through the second hole.

His eyes and cheeks are made from scraps of coloured paper, or felt glued into position. His mouth is drawn in felt tip-ped pen, practice first with pencil.

2 Arthur's hat is made from a strip of tan felt measuring about 13 by 4 cm.

Fold the felt in half and in matching thread, sew the two ends together about half way down. Then in similar running stitches, sew all the way round the long edge and leave the threads long.

Pull the threads together to gather the felt into a hat shape, then firmly oversew the end and turn the right side out.

When glued on Arthur's head, the wire fits through this gap.

3 Arthur's "appendages" are petal shaped pieces cut out of the tan felt (9 pieces in all will be needed).

Sew 5 of these petal shaped appendages together in a bunch, then glue them to the top of Arthur's hat.

Then glue 2 more petal-shaped pieces under Arthur's chin.

4 Arthur's body is made up in sections. Cut out small circles of the tan felt and sew all round the edge in small running stitches (leave the ends of the thread long).

Pull the threads to gather into a pouch and then with cotton wool or tissue as stuffing, shape into a small cushion. Oversew the end very firmly and fasten off.

Squash the pouch into a flatter shape and then with a bradawl or pointed scissors make a hole right through the middle of the section. With the gathered side down, thread the section onto the wire and push up to the head.

5 Arthur's arms are a length of the wire about 15 cm long and looped in the middle. The hands are shapes cut from black paper or card and glued at each end.

Thread the arms into position and then continue making body sections as before.

Thread 8 more of these onto the wire and then twist the spare wire at the end into a flat loop. This can be hidden under the gathered edge of the last section.

Make one final cushion but do not make a hole in it. Glue the gathered side of this, to the last section on the wire to complete Arthur's body.

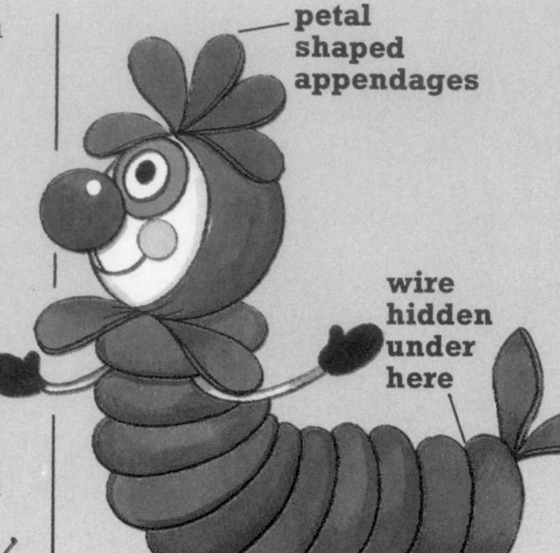

Bend Arthur to shape, so that he sits up properly. You may need to experiment a little to get the balance right.

Arthur is now very nearly finished.

Add the finishing touch by sewing the last 2 petal shapes of tan coloured felt together, and then gluing them to the top end of the last body section, as shown here.

Arthur is now complete.

Evil Edna

1 Evil Edna is made from an old grocery packet, something like a suet box will do. The one that we used measured 11.5 x 8.5 cm.

Begin by covering the box neatly, all over in dark grey paper. Take care not to get glue on the outside of the covered box.

grey paper

2 Next in the light grey paper cut out the TV screen. (Ours measured 9 x 7.5 cm). Round off the corners neatly to give the correct shape. Before you stick this into position it is much easier to first complete the detail on Edna's face.

Draw carefully in pencil first and then when you have got the expression just right, draw in black felt pen. Complete the finer details with yellow and white paper for the eyes and teeth.

When Edna's face is complete, (make sure the ink is dry so it does not smudge) carefully glue it into position leaving space for the control knobs.

3 The aerial is very simply a piece of wire pushed into a domed tap washer and bent into shape as below.

Then carefully glue the completed aerial to the top of the box, as below.

aerial

domed tap washer

grocery packet

coloured paper glued to leg

Use the glue sparingly and avoid spilling excess glue on the model.

4 The 3 large control knobs are buttons covered with discs of the dark grey coloured paper. Use the buttons as a pattern to draw round, then cut out the grey paper circles and glue them on to the buttons.

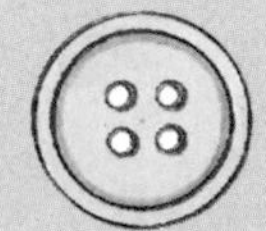

The smaller control knobs are simply cut out of the light grey paper and glued into position below the other knobs.

5 Evil Edna's legs are made from narrow strips of strong cardboard (we used the corrugated kind) glued together to make a double thickness. For the legs cut 4 lengths about 5 cm long.

Then make 4 shorter lengths about 3.5 cm long for Edna's feet.

Glue the foot on to one end of the leg piece and open out the other end a little way.

Finally cover the sides of the feet and legs with strips of blue and white paper.

leg

foot

OUTSTANDING ENDEAVOUR

Five chart-busting boys from Birmingham hit the headlines last year when they became the youngest-ever band to reach number one in the ratings! *Pass the Dutchie* brought fame and fortune to 11-year old Kelvin Grant and his 13-year old brother Michael, 15-year old Junior and 14-year old Patrick Waite, and 15-year old Dennis Seaton, but in spite of the glamour of becoming pop stars, the boys never forgot the support they had from their school – Duddeston Manor.

'We get a lot of help from the teachers,' Dennis told us when Musical Youth made their first appearance on Blue Peter, and to show their appreciation, Musical Youth put on a concert especially to raise funds to build a garage for the school mini-bus.

We chose Musical Youth to win our Blue Peter Award for Outstanding Endeavour, not only for their incredible achievement in the tough and competitive world of rock music, but because, unlike some bands, they *didn't* let success go to their heads! And it's not a flash in the pan, either. *Pass the Dutchie* reached No. 10 in America, and *Never Gonna Give You Up*, went to No 6 in the British charts.

You might think the boys would be big-headed after all their successes and their tours of Britain, Europe and the USA, but not a bit of it. It's hard work and talent that's got them to the top – in other words, Outstanding Endeavour!

THE CALL OF THE WILD

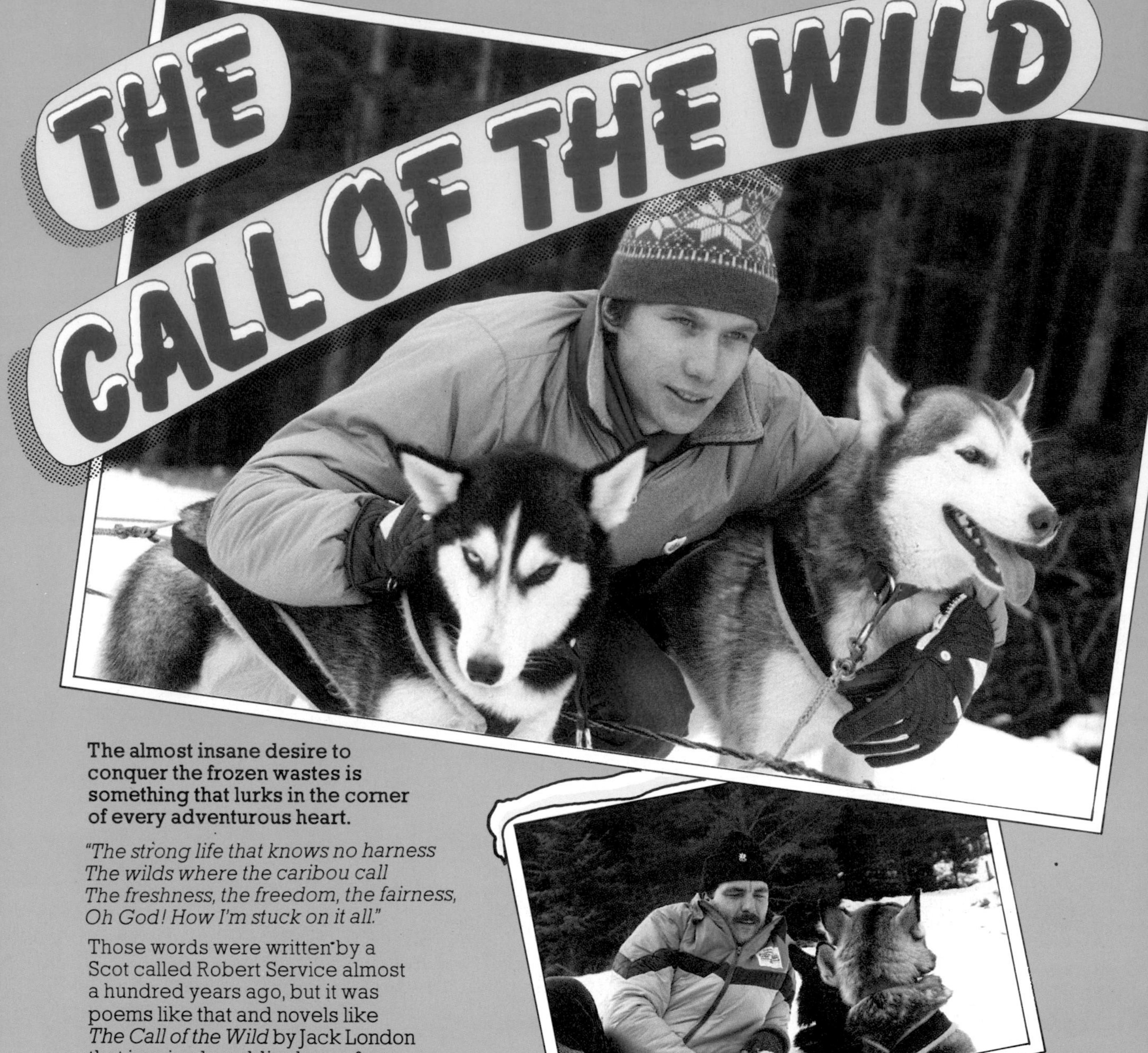

The almost insane desire to conquer the frozen wastes is something that lurks in the corner of every adventurous heart.

"The strong life that knows no harness
The wilds where the caribou call
The freshness, the freedom, the fairness,
Oh God! How I'm stuck on it all."

Those words were written by a Scot called Robert Service almost a hundred years ago, but it was poems like that and novels like *The Call of the Wild* by Jack London that inspired a soldier home from the Falklands to become the first Briton to compete in what must be the most gruelling and terrifying race in the world – the North American Husky Dog Open Championships at Fairbanks in Alaska.

This is a 70-mile Dog Sledge race across the most rugged country in the North Polar Region. It lasts for three days, with temperatures as low as 30 degrees below zero. The soldier's name is Gareth Pugh and he competed with hard men who'd spent a lifetime with dogs and sledges in the most desperate part of the world. Gareth was unabashed when I met him – but I suppose a man who had taken part in the San Carlos landings and the Battle for Port Stanley in the Falklands war, doesn't scare that easily. I was able to share in the first part of Gareth's training . . . not in the Polar Zone exactly, but in the north of Scotland where Gareth had his very first lesson in handling a Dog Sled team.

It was there that we met John Evans, a tough, stocky man with a beard, wearing a trapper's fur hat. He was driving towards us through a great, white wake of snow, yelling "Hike on – hike on, Natasha – Hike on Saba."

The dogs all had Russian names, and the first sight of them bounding through the snow stops your heart. They are beautiful and powerful, frightening and cuddly all at the same time. Their coat is so thick it looks like fur, even the insides of ears are lined with thick hair. John showed us that their feet are webbed, which helps them to grip on the powdered snow.

The sledges are basic to say the least. The runners extend backwards with enough room to take your feet. In the middle there is a crude snow-plough brake.

"Very important to stop you over-running the dogs on the downhill stretches," John told us.

The two handles help you to steer by lifting the runners from the snow. "Lift the left and you veer to the right. Lift the right and you veer to the left."

I joined Gareth Pugh, who was training to be the first Briton to take part in the North American Husky Dog Open Championships.

Our instructor was John Evans.

Natasha, Mujinda and Saba – harnessed and ready to pull me across the snow.

John has been involved with huskies for eight years. He loves them and respects their courage and their staying power.

"A 16-dog team like you'll have in Alaska," he told Gareth, "will pull a man for 50 miles through a blizzard with only the occasional stop for food.

"Like a fuel stop?" said Gareth.

"It's more than that," he replied. "The great secret of a dog team is the relationship between the driver and the dogs. And the way to a Husky's heart is through his stomach!"

John had provided food for the teams that Gareth and I were going to drive, but he insisted that we each fed our own team.

"You do something for them – and they'll do something for you," he said.

My team comprised of two beautiful black and white bitches called Natasha and Mujinda, and a magnificent brown-red dog called Saba. Gareth had three bitches, Natalya, Nadine and Boryshna. But before we harnessed up the dogs, John gave us a lesson in sledge handling by having us run down a steep hill without dogs. Gareth and I started by running behind the sledges until they gathered speed on the hill and then we leapt onto the foot rests – rather like bob-sleighers. The snow was hard-packed and I soon began to pick up speed. In no time at all the track swung sharply to the right. I threw all my weight on to my right foot and lifted the left-hand runner. A huge fir tree came hurtling towards me and I felt the needles brush my face as my runner shaved the roots and I bucketted on down the hill. At the foot of the hill was the frozen, glassy expanse of Loch Morlich which took us both by surprise. We bumped off the track and on to the ice, and immediately accelerated over the smooth surface of the Loch. I put down a foot to steady myself – and that was fatal. I went one way

I soon discovered there was more to Dog Sledge racing than meets the eye!

Our training session ended with a neck-and-neck race along the frozen shores of Loch Morlich.

and the sledge went the other. I eventually came to rest in a bundle of arms and legs which turned out to be Gareth who had done the same thing!

That was our first lesson. Never get separated from the sledge.

"When you've got 16 dogs in full cry, they won't stop for you or for anybody," warned John.

The dogs will always go in a straight line, but they are not like a team of horses with reins and bits to steer them. They will stick to the track, but the problems occur when the track gets blurred by snow and the dogs just keep on going, missing out all the bends.

Gareth and I had an individual lesson on dog handling. I had always heard the Eskimos in the pictures shout "Mush" to get their team moving. But John told us there are only two commands: "Hike on!" – not "Mush" – gets the team moving, and "Whoa!" makes them stop.

"It's the encouragement you give them that motivates the team," John told us. "You've got to keep on calling their names and lifting their hearts!"

John was quite pleased with the way we'd picked up the rudiments of sledging and he suggested that we should end up by having a race against each other. "It will give you a taste of competition sledging," John told Gareth.

We both made a fuss of our dogs. I told Natasha and Mujinda that they were the most beautiful huskies in the world, and Saba was the most powerful. He responded by putting his nose in the air and giving the most spine-chilling "Call of the wild" howl which echoed across the Loch. They're great actors, these dogs.

We lined up with our teams and John counted us down for the start. "Hike on!" I yelled, and the sledge began to move.

Gareth made a good start as well and for the first 50 metres we were almost neck and neck. "Come on Natasha – Saba – Saba – hike on!" The track narrowed as we approached a bend. It was obvious that there was only enough room for one sledge at the apex of the corner.

"Hike on!" – my voice echoed across the snow and was answered by an equally lusty "Hike on!" from Gareth – but he was drawing away from me. "Come on, Saba," I yelled, and began to lean in to take the corner. But Gareth had the edge – he was half a length ahead now and in position for the bend. With a great flurry of snow he put his sledge into a broadside – and from then on all I could see was the back of his sledge as he drove to the winning post.

Although I'm a natural competitior – which means I play every game to win – I was glad that it was Gareth who had pipped me to the post on that occasion. After all, it was he who had answered "the Call of the Wild" and was going to make that long journey to the Polar Zone to join the hard men in the most gruelling race that has ever been invented.

"There's the land. Have you seen it?
It's the cussedness land that I know.
From the big, dizzy mountains
that screen it, To the deep,
deathlike valleys below."

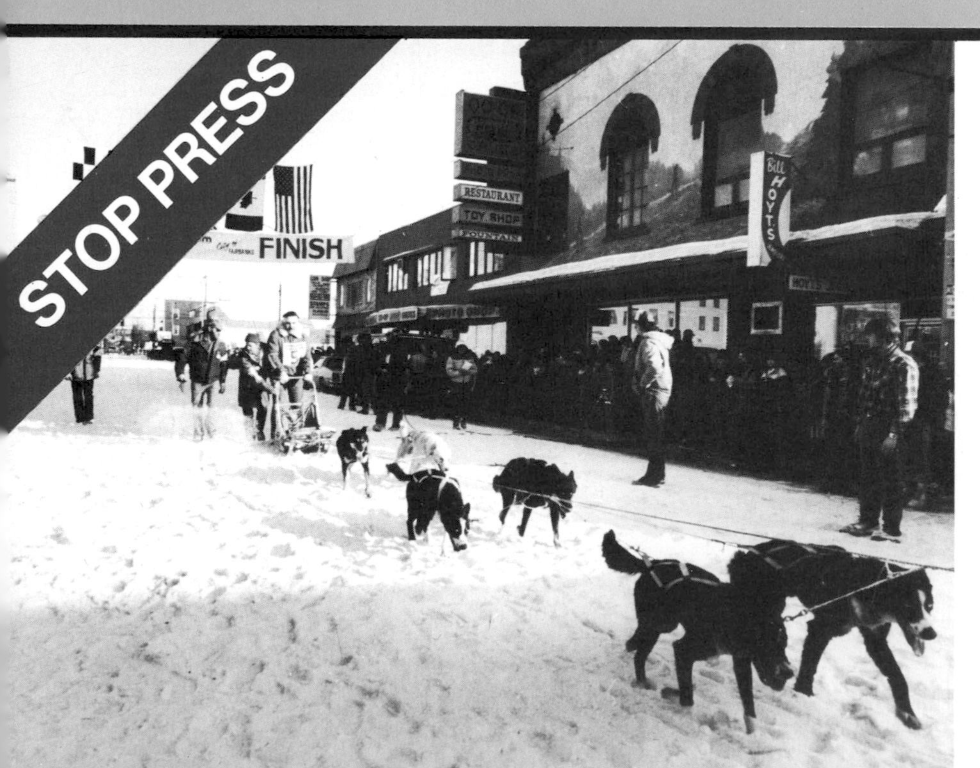

STOP PRESS:
Well, of course, we didn't leave it there. Four days later we booked a telephone call to Alaska to find out how Gareth had got on in the big race. And the great news was that he had come 13th out of a field of nineteen. When you realise that Gareth was racing against men who have spent a lifetime in the frozen north, it was no mean achievement. Gareth told us that the main difference between the race and our training in Scotland was cold and speed. It was down 20 below in Alaska, and the 16 dog team bombed him along at speeds of up to 30 mph. His greatest fear was falling off, because the dogs wouldn't wait for him – and as Gareth put it, "it would have been a pretty long walk back . . .!"

BOWLED OVER!

The Chelsea Pensioners, upright proud old soldiers in scarlet coats and tricorn hats, are one of the famous sights of London as they walk proudly down the King's Road in Chelsea, mingling with the tourists and the trendy shoppers.

The King's Road is called after *their* king – King Charles the Second, who founded the Royal Hospital where they live, over 300 years ago.

In the 18th century, the word hospital meant a place of refuge, not somewhere to go when you're ill, as it does today. In fact, most of the old soldiers I met were far from being sick. Fighting fit is how I would describe them! James Kain was 98: "I'm looking forward to the Queen's telegram for my 100th birthday in 18 months time". But he was a mere boy compared with William Hisland, the Royal Hospital's record breaker, who died in 1732 aged 112!

King Charles had a special friend called Nell Gwynne, who was an actress from the Theatre Royal, Drury Lane, which is still there today. The story goes that King Charles offered Nell a gift of land in Chelsea, but she refused it, telling the king to use it to build a home for his old soldiers. Whether this happened or not, it is certainly true that Charles told Sir Christopher Wren, the man who built St. Paul's Cathedral, to start work on a hospital for old soldiers in 1682.

Wren designed not only one of the most beautiful buildings in London, but a place tailor-made for old soldiers to live in. The staircases have wide, shallow steps for the elderly men to walk up in safety, and if they get a bit out of puff half way up, there's a built-in bench on each landing so that they can get their breath back before tackling the next flight. Each pensioner has his own private room, called a berth, which is on a wide corridor called a Long Ward. About every ten metres along the ward there are a series of sitting places with a coffee table and a group of easy chairs, so that the soldiers can sit together and gossip or play cards, but they can go back to the privacy of their own room when the fancy takes them. There is a gap between the top of the wall and the ceiling, big enough for a man to climb over in case one of the old men should fall and hurt himself after he had locked the door. Wren seems to have thought of everything.

Christopher Wren remembered he was building for old soldiers, and he put seats on the landings.

I was escorted to Room No. 4 on one of the long wards to meet Mr. Martin Wager, formerly Squadron Quarter-Master Corporal Wager of the Life Guards. His room was like an army museum, the walls covered with pictures of soldiers, some in scarlet and gold dress uniforms, some wearing pit helmets and khaki drill in a faraway corner of the old British Empire. Dominating the room was a photograph of an exceptionally handsome young life guard who bore a strong resemblance to the

Mr Wager proudly showed me the souvenirs of a lifetime spent in the Army.

equally handsome, if now not exceptionally young, occupant of Room No. 4. "That was me – at the age of 18," he said proudly. There was a colour photograph, more recently taken, of Mr. Wager and another pensioner in their scarlet tunics, standing stiffly to attention and each carrying a halberd in their right hands.

"That's myself and my friend. We are the Halberdiers. We are the only two who carry the halberds on Founders Day, and this year we shall be escorting Her Majesty the Queen."

He was obviously a modest man, but the pride in his eyes and in his voice was unmistakable. It is wonderful to think that after a lifetime of service, Mr. Wager's moment was going to happen when he reached his eighties.

Founders Day is the great day when each year, on May 20th, the In-Pensioners as they are called, celebrate their founder, Charles II's birthday. It is also called Oak Apple Day because when Charles was a young man there was a revolution in England. Oliver Cromwell was in command and the king was on the run with a price on his head. His father had been beheaded by Cromwell and Charles knew he could expect no mercy if he was caught. Once he escaped capture by hiding for hours in an oak tree whilst the Roundheads searched the ground below.

Only two pensioners carry the halberds.

King Charles was, in time, restored to the throne and made a triumphant entry into London on May 20th, 1660 – his thirtieth birthday. Everyone wore bunches of oak leaves and cheered him to the echo.

Now, every 20th May, the In-Pensioners parade, each man wearing a sprig of oak leaves, and the statue of their founder is shrouded in oak

James Kain, a sprightly 98, was the oldest of the In-Pensioners.

The Queen stands before the statue of Charles II, which is decked in oak leaves on Founders Day.

branches to commemorate the day his life was saved by an oak tree. Around the court, about the statue, are painted these words in latin: "IN SUBSIDIUM ET LEVAMEN, EMERITORUM SENIO BELLOQUE FRACTORUM, CONDIDIT CAROLUS SECUNDUS" which means that this building was founded by Charles the Second for the relief and comfort of old soldiers, weakened by age or broken by war.

An old soldier who seemed far from weakened by age or broken by war was the great-grandfather of Blue Peter badge holders Sharon and Karl Speed who had written asking me to look their great-grandpa up when I went to the Hospital. I met him on the bowling green, having a game with a bunch of his friends and they asked me to join in.

Karl Speed and his great-grandfather.

I'd never played bowls before, which is a very skilled game, but Great-grandpa Briggs very patiently told me how to hold the "wood" and where to aim. I'm very glad we were filming because no-one would have believed what happened without the evidence of the camera. I bowled a perfect wood! "A toucher" was how George Briggs described it. I wouldn't play any more after that – because I reckon that's one for the record books. I was probably the first woman to play bowls in the Royal Hospital, anyway – but to bowl a toucher . . . !

King Charles sadly didn't live to see his hospital completed, but he did see what is perhaps the most beautiful part in all its glory – the Chapel, made by Wren, the greatest builder of English churches to this day.

On the altar are two candlesticks given to the hospital by Charles' brother, King James the Second. The matching cross that stands between them was given by Charles' cousin ten times removed, our present Queen Elizabeth II.

King Charles II and his friend, Nell Gwynne.

Every Sunday the In-Pensioners assemble for Church Parade and file into the chapel for morning service, and every Sunday for 300 years, King Charles has been remembered by this special prayer:

"O God, who by the overshadowing of an oak didst preserve our Royal Founder from the hand of his enemies and so lead him to an earthly throne, grant thy heavenly protection, we beseech thee, to thy servants in this Royal Hospital, that continuing in thy love, they may give thee true and loyal service, and so enduring to the end, enter at the last into thine eternal kingdom in glory, through the merits of Jesus Christ Our Lord and Saviour."

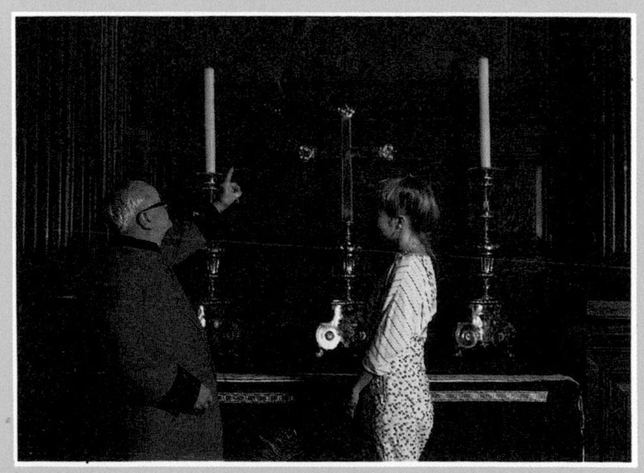

This silver cross was given by our Queen.

PUZZLE PICTURES

1 A replica of the famous **Montgolfier Balloon** which made the first manned flight 200 years ago.

2 The colossal teddy that was given to our **Treasure Hunt Appeal** by the children of Summerfield School, Bath.

3 The **7th Tonbridge Eden Valley Pack** exchanged their Cub Scout uniforms for Father Christmas outfits to go carol singing in aid of our Treasure Hunt.

4 Two of an amazing litter of **one-eared rabbits** from Mrs. Lockwood's Donkey Centre in Surrey.

5 **Ann Droid** created by Mr. Holland of Hemel Hempstead to

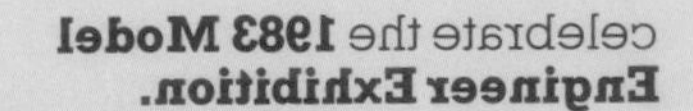

celebrate the **1983 Model Engineer Exhibition.**

6 **Philip Berent** brought his single seater **Microlight aircraft** to the studio before his attempted journey of 11,000 miles from Wiltshire to Zimbabwe.

7 **Blue Peter Guide Dogs Buttons and Prince**, with their owners Elsie Whitehead and John Bates, joined us for a preview of the **Natural History Museum's special exhibition for blind and partially-sighted people.**

8 **The world's first inflatable disco.**

9 **Jack Bennett**, ex-crew member of HMS Vanguard, who helps move our Blue Peter scenery, and the magnificent **1/96 scale model** of HMS Vanguard built by Mr. Alex MacFadyen.

THE CASE OF THE BULLET TRAIN MYSTERY

1 Jolly said there was nothing he liked better than to get his boots on the table and have a natter. But as Bob remarked, you would never, ever, wear shoes in the house in Japan. He could hardly know Japan well if he made such a mistake.

2 Jolly said he lived in the historic centre of Tokyo. But as Bob said, Tokyo is a recent city, and is all modern.

3 Jolly said he was an expert in trains, but also said that a bullet train's top speed was 100 miles per hour. Bob and McCann had already seen that the speedometer in the buffet car read 210 kilometres an hour – 130 miles an hour.

4 Jolly said the Japanese invented the name bullet train. But Bob and McCann knew that the Japanese have a different name for the trains. An expert in Japan must have known this, so plainly Jolly was an impostor.

5 Jolly said he walked for five minutes on the platform. As Bob and McCann saw, the trains stop for a very short time and Jolly would have had no chance for his stroll. This was obviously a desperate lie from some-one not used to Japan.

6 Jolly said he had not been to England for ten years – yet he had a ticket stub in his pocket for the Hallam Big Band Extravaganza, a new show in London Bob was anxious to see. Again, Jolly was caught in a lie.

Useful Information

Ditchley Dress
National Portrait Gallery,
2 St Martin's Place, London WC2

British Balloon and Airship Club
4 Pound Lane, Fishponds, Bristol

Royal Hospital Chelsea
London SW3
Open: Monday–Saturday
1000–1200 hrs. 1400–1600 hrs.
Sunday and Bank Holidays
1400–1600 hrs.

Canadian High Commission
Canada House, Trafalgar Square,
London SW1

Phillips
7 Blenheim Street, New Bond Street,
London W1

Roadline UK Ltd
The Merton Centre,
45 St. Peter's Street,
Bedford MK40 8UB

Scottish Parcel Services Ltd
Hillview Road,
East Tullos,
Aberdeen AB9 2DQ

Northern Ireland Carriers Ltd
Grosvenor Road,
Belfast BT12 5AX

Acknowledgements

Co-ordinator:
Gillian Farnsworth

Designed by **Glyn Davies** assisted by **Philip Gilderdale, Kathy Gammon, Linda Newsham, Tim Scott**

Prince Albert's Greyhound was written by **Dorothy Smith** and illustrated by **Robert Broomfield**

Wigs, Wobbley Bobblies, Willo the Wisp and *Crispy Mince Pies* by **Margaret Parnell**

The Case of the Bullet Train Mystery was written by **Simon Barnes**

Illustrations were by Robert Broomfield, David Brown, Selwyn Hutchinson, Alan Burton, Lisa Jenson, Bill Lefeure, Sarah Silcox, Tony Spaul

All photographs were taken by Joan Williams, David Clarke, John Jefford, Robert Hill, Barry Boxall, Ian Oliver and Conrad Hafenrichter with the exception of:
Landseer painting (p.29) by gracious permission of H.M. The Queen; Guy the Gorilla (p.33) by Zoological Society of London; photograph p.39 and top right p.63 by Mary Evans Picture Library; Ditchley Dress (p.59) by National Portrait Gallery; Finish of race (p.72) by Smirnhoff Vodka; painting (top right p.75) by Victoria and Albert Museum, Crown Copyright.

SILVER JUBILEE COMPETITION

Do you recognise these pictures? They're the covers of all our Blue Peter Annuals and you can see them enlarged at the back and front of this edition. If you know which cover belongs to which book – for example, Cover F is the 19th Book – this could be your chance to meet Goldie, Jack and the Blue Peter Team at a special

25th BIRTHDAY PARTY

Write your answers on the official entry form and send it to:
Blue Peter
Silver Jubilee Competition
BBC TV Centre,
London W12 7RJ

First prize winners and runners-up will be notified by letter.
Closing date: 10 January 1984

1 Q	**6**	**11** R	**16** C
2	**7**	**12** J	**17** N
3	**8**	**13** G	**18** S
4	**9**	**14** K	**19** F
5	**10**	**15** P	

Name ....

Address ....

....

....

....

Age ....

SPOT THE COVER!

For details of an exciting competition for our Silver Jubilee edition, and the chance to meet Goldie, Jack and the Blue Peter Team, turn back to page 77 and fill in the coupon.

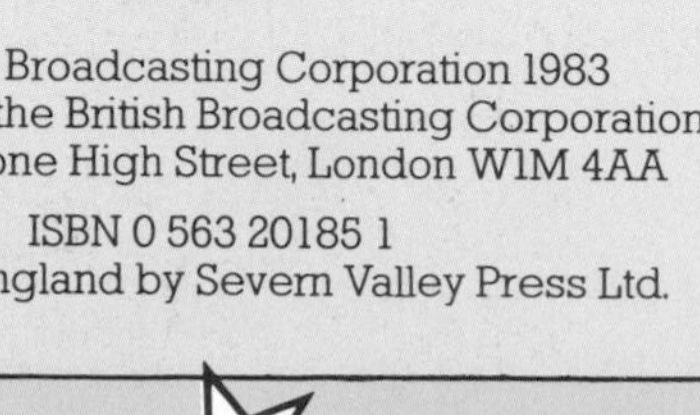

Published by the British Broadcasting Corporation
35 Marylebone High Street, London W1M 4AA

ISBN 0 563 20185 1
Printed in England by Severn Valley Press Ltd.